RECONCILIATION VIA THE WAR CRIMES TRIBUNAL?

Reconciliation via the War Crimes Tribunal?

ALEKSANDAR FATIĆ
Senior Fellow
Institute of International Politics and Economics, Belgrade
President
The Management Center, Belgrade

LONDON AND NEW YORK

First published 2000 by Ashgate Publishing

Reissued 2018 by Routledge
2 Park Square, Milton Park, Abingdon, Oxon, OX14 4RN
711 Third Avenue, New York, NY 10017, USA

Routledge is an imprint of the Taylor & Francis Group, an informa business

Copyright © Aleksandar Fatić 2000

All rights reserved. No part of this book may be reprinted or reproduced or utilised in any form or by any electronic, mechanical, or other means, now known or hereafter invented, including photocopying and recording, or in any information storage or retrieval system, without permission in writing from the publishers.

Notice:
Product or corporate names may be trademarks or registered trademarks, and are used only for identification and explanation without intent to infringe.

Publisher's Note
The publisher has gone to great lengths to ensure the quality of this reprint but points out that some imperfections in the original copies may be apparent.

Disclaimer
The publisher has made every effort to trace copyright holders and welcomes correspondence from those they have been unable to contact.

A Library of Congress record exists under LC control number: 99075545

ISBN 13: 978-0-367-00037-0 (hbk)
ISBN 13: 978-0-367-00038-7 (pbk)
ISBN 13: 978-0-429-44485-2 (ebk)

Contents

Preface vii

Introduction 1

1 The Background and Diplomatic Significance of the ICTY 5

2 The Nature of the Peace in the Former Yugoslavia: Heroes and Criminals — How to Distinguish Them? 12

3 The Political Landscape of Peace in the Balkans 34

4 The ICTY's Aspirations, its Statute, and Some of the Legal Inconsistencies in its Establishment 45

5 The First Indictments and What They Show 58

6 Crimes and Responsibility in a Civil War 71

7 Policy Issues 81

8 NATO and the ICTY 90

Bibliography *107*

Preface

This book was being finished in the Spring of 1999. It was being written for a British publisher with whom I had already cooperated extensively, in the Serbian capital of Belgrade, while NATO bombs were falling on the city and air raid sirens interrupted the writing for hours and days at a time.

Explosions were heard in close proximity while casual chat went on with neighbors, shop-attendants, and people hurrying to the shelters with small children and blankets in their arms.

The conversations in the long hours under air raid emergency regime sometimes wandered off in strange directions, yet ones that seemed so natural. People compared their lives and situations to those of the citizens of London during the Second World War. Theatres throughout the city played free of charge or for a token fee, even during the air raid alerts. They bore signs at the entrances saying "Shelter of the free spirit".

Not a few hundred kilometers from the city, hundreds of thousands of civilians had left their homes and become refugees. At the same time, civilian settlements, towns and villages throughout the country were being destroyed by "stray bombs", as western politicians liked to call them. Scores of soldiers and civilians were being buried across Serbia. The Kosovo capital of Priština was being demolished through a combination of NATO bombing and ground battles between the police and the army on the one side, and the troops of the rebel "Kosovo Liberation Army" (KLA) — probably fairly describable as the Yugoslav equivalent of the IRA or the Red Brigades, on the other side.

One night during the writing of this preface, the Gračanica Monastery, the oldest and holiest of all Serbian Orthodox monasteries, was damaged by an airborne missile. Poisonous fumes from chemical factories around Belgrade spread to the city after the factories were hit from the air.

Media reports indicate that during the odd seventy days of the war hundreds of thousands of people have become displaced and dispossessed in Kosovo. Human suffering on both sides in the conflict, Serbian and Albanian, has reached new heights. On one side, a political impasse has created ground for a military intervention. On the other side, the military intervention has changed the political avenues for negotiation in ways that are not necessarily favorable or conducive to a good or just settlement. As in any war, confusion reigns and the misery of those who are the weakest is the greatest.

The above lines are not simply the records of a war. It is rather a sketch of the circumstances in the midst of which final touches are added to this book. Such circumstances place one in a particular emotional and intellectual situation. They generate a feeling that the concurrent diplomatic and military activities fly in the face of each other, and that any discussion of international justice appears meaningless where force is used as the ultimate argument in the solving of regional crises. At the same time, one wonders where things would go without international justice, and what kind of justice it ought to be — what principles it should adopt, who its judges should be, and who would decide on the question of whether international courts act prudently or not. Clearly, crises like this one require international justice, but a blindfolded justice indeed it must be, otherwise the region of southeastern Europe would be better off without international judicial intervention. A justice that is mixed with diplomacy in the sense that it serves the purposes of those who have a greater force at their disposal, would hardly be a justice at all. Yet, many in the region of southeastern Europe believe that the International Tribunal for the Former Yugoslavia administers just such a type of justice. It is this perception that hinders the meting out of justice, and it is the management of this perception, as well as the discussion of its foundations, that is the subject of this book.

The contention of this book is that the future of the ICTY, and of any other international war crimes tribunal, will be decided by its responses to challenges of impartiality and judicial consistency. If the ICTY reacts vigorously to defend its independence, and if in its actions after the latest Balkan war it brings forward indictments of all those responsible for civilian deaths and breaches of international humanitarian law, it stands a good chance of becoming the bedrock of an entrenched and integrated system of international justice for war crimes. If, on the other hand, the actions of the ICTY remain at least perceivedly biased and aligned with western diplomacy, then the ICTY may well bury the future of international justice for war crimes for a long time to come.

This book deals with public international law from a political, diplomatic, humanitarian and strategic points of view. It was written over the period of two years at several institutions in Australia, Britain, and FR Yugoslavia. I acknowledge with gratitude the support this work has received in various stages of its completion, by the Research Support Scheme in Prague, the Ian Potter Foundation in Melbourne, the Friedrich

Ebert Stiftung in Belgrade, and by the University of South Australia in Adelaide, which generously granted me a semester-long leave from teaching in 1997 to work on this book. The book was completed in the course of my normal research and analytic work at the Institute of International Politics and Economics in Belgrade. I am deeply grateful to those closest to me, whose generosity and support have made work on this book possible.

Aleksandar Fatić, Belgrade, 16 June 1999

Introduction

The International Criminal Tribunal for the Former Yugoslavia (ICTY), operating under the auspices of the United Nations, serves the role of applying international judicial measures as a form of outside intervention aimed to effect at least three goals:

(1) Bring those guilty of war crimes to answer for their actions, and thus fulfill moral and legal justice,
(2) Help stabilize the peace in the former Yugoslavia by affirming the principle of individual guilt for war time atrocities, as opposed to the guilt of entire nations, and
(3) Help effect a reconciliation between the nations torn apart by war.

The third goal is arguably the most important one, because it is only a comprehensive reconciliation in southeastern Europe that can facilitate political, economic and social progress and a stabilization of the security situation in the entire region.

The thrust of the argument of this book is in the need to view the development of the security crises in the former Yugoslavia primarily as a result of *avoidable actions and faults* of political elites, rather than as an unavoidable "spreading" of ethnic conflict after the "collapse" of communism in eastern Europe. In normal circumstances, I would argue for a legal and legitimate international action against the elites that "run" wars, whose fault the killings are, rather than on the region's stated "historical determinism" in ethnic confrontation.

For almost more than a decade of crises in the Balkans, a few western nations that like to call themselves "the international community" have systematically failed to recognize the responsibility of the elites, and have instead subscribed to a fatalistic "no-fault view of history".[1] Such a view contributed to continued killing where human tragedies *could have been avoided* by decisive diplomatic measures taken against the elites. I argue that such decisive action against the powerful individuals, not just in the former Yugoslavia, but also in the "international community", could and would have stopped the wars much sooner. I argue that such actions, however difficult and, sometimes, associated with what seems as prohibitive political costs, would have to be taken by an appropriate future international court in order for peace in southeastern Europe to take hold, and for reconciliation and forgiveness to start taking place.

During the 52nd session of the United Nations' Commission for Human Rights in Geneva, on 16 April 1996, Elizabeth Rehn, the UN Secretary General's special envoy for human rights in the former Yugoslavia, protested against ascriptions of collective guilt to entire nations for crimes committed by individuals. In doing so, she invoked the principle that the ICTY had sought to uphold by its very mission: the need to effect a catharsis of accumulated feelings of ethnic hatred that arise from unclear conceptions of responsibility for the atrocities committed during civil wars.

When individual responsibility is either unclear by itself, or deliberately obscured, it tends to be increasingly seen as *collective*. By clearly identifying the guilty individuals and penalizing them for their crimes, an international war crimes tribunal may hope to facilitate a de-escalation of tensions and animosities between the ethnic collectives, and encourage a rapprochement between the formerly warring nations. From the political and social point of view, this was the most important mission of the ICTY. So far, the ICTY has failed in fulfilling this mission badly.

From a legal point of view, it is essential to bring those guilty of war crimes to justice, because only in that way can moral standards and the basic criteria of legitimate behavior be re-established in the war-torn states of the region. While the fighting goes on, chaos reigns in all the territories infested with warfare, and the civil, political and legal institutions charged with the protection of civil standards and human rights tend to be destroyed or severely compromised in their integrity and efficiency.

The aim of this book is to address some of the critical conceptual and practical issues facing the ICTY and offer practical suggestions as to how these controversies would have to be addressed by international actors and any future international war crimes tribunals after the Yugoslav civil wars, and during and after most future civil wars.

The ICTY is not only a judicial body. It is a result of diplomacy, and its work follows diplomacy in the sense that, as an international court, it depends on diplomacy in the sense that the feasibility of all of its actions is conditioned by what international diplomacy can deliver.

I try to be critical here of all the policies and actions, whoever they might be committed by, that constitute violations of human rights and accepted rules of conduct both internally and internationally. Such actions include violence, and the world has witnessed that in the Balkans in the

1990s all sides, both local and those acting on behalf of the leading powers of the world, have resorted to violence. The book discusses the diplomatic and legal aspects of the ICTY, the credibility issues that surround it, strategies involved in its mission, and its relationship with the role of the UN and NATO in the crisis management efforts in southeastern Europe. This last topic demonstrates the strategic and operations role the ICTY plays in maintaining peace and security in Europe. With the Kosovo crisis breaking out into the open in 1999, and with the newest, highly intensified activities of the ICTY that are connected with the pronounced role that NATO has started to play in FRY, the relationship between the ICTY and NATO has become an inescapable question. This is why the considerations of diplomatic and legal aspects of the ICTY's work here conclude with a consideration of the relationship between peace in southeastern Europe and the politics of both NATO and FR Yugoslavia, for it is these relations that constitute the political and strategic stage on which the ICTY performs and defines its ever evolving role.

Finally, a semantic remark. Throughout the book, I refer to the "international community" in quotation marks. This is not because I intend any a priori critical connotation to the term, but because I feel somewhat uneasy about it. The term "international community" suggests a majority of nations, a majority of the world's people, and the broadest conceivable international agenda. In reality, this is not what is meant by the "international community". The term is used to refer to the world's most powerful countries, which are few, and whose populations fall far short of being the majority. Their agenda is also not the broadest possible one. While, admittedly, these countries lead the world today, and in that sense their actions are largely causally operative for the shape of contemporary international relations, they are not, in my judgment, the international community. They may be an international community belonging to a group of several such communities, and they may be the dominant one. They are spoken of frequently in the course of the book because they are so important, but they are referred to in quotation marks to suggest an uneasiness about considering them the only international community that there is.

In the last year of its work, I have seen the ICTY start to act increasingly according to the strategic alternatives that had been erected in the unfinished manuscript of this book. The work on developing those options and strategies thus assumed a dynamic nature as facts on which they were based changed and developed. A certain "delay" has been left between the facts on which the anticipations and conclusions of the book are founded and the anticipated or emerging realities as the manuscript goes to print. This has been done to test the assumptions and conclusions of the argument according to how the world will look and what the ICTY's prospects will be after this text is truly born out of the printing press.

Note

1   See Brown, M.E. (ed.), *The international dimensions of internal conflict*, MIT Press, Cambridge, Mass., 1996, "Introduction", pp. 1–32.

1 The Background and Diplomatic Significance of the ICTY

The international diplomatic landscape that was shaped by the massacres of the Bosnian and Croatian wars contained dramatic novelties compared to the realm of traditional European diplomacy before the violent disintegration of the former Yugoslavia. The era of international relations that had started after the end of the Cold War had been marked by contradictory trends: an increasing integration, and a violent political, territorial, and cultural fragmentation and disintegration; an increasing insistence on multilateralism and the peaceful settlement of disputes by diplomatic means on the one hand, and the use of violence to promote the goals and interests of the newly established hierarchies of global dominance, on the other.

There are convincing examples of both. While the European Union has by now achieved an unprecedented degree of coherence in the history of European integration, countries such as the former Yugoslavia and the former Soviet Union have entered a viciously violent inferno of disintegration and murderous quest for national statehood. While the large international organizations, first of all the system of the United Nations with its subsystems, have assumed a leading role in international affairs and imposed the demands of multilateral diplomatic legitimization on all of its members, motivated by the principles of non-violence and respect for the equal rights of others, the great powers of the newly created world of international relations have used exceeding violence against third countries. This has been done ostensibly to impose the principles of peace and international cooperation, but in reality it has mostly been motivated by their desire to secure various types of hegemony on a global level.

The Security Council of the United Nations has become the most important global diplomatic decision-making body that decides the matters of war and peace throughout the world. At the same time, the United States of America and its allies have conducted military attacks, legitimized by the political decisions taken in the UN Security Council during the 1990s, against Iraq and the military positions of Bosnian Serbs. The amount of aggression that has been applied in the name of multilateralism in international relations and global peace has, so to say, reached a level that is a major threat to countries that do not have a place at the multilateral decision-making table within the large international organizations.

Diplomacy has been, and is, the major tool whereby countries, great and small alike, have fought for a place at that table. Some have been more successful than others. Those countries that do not appropriately participate in the work of the UN system, the OSCE, the EU, SECI and other global and regional organizations, face the unattractive prospect of being the object of policy of international organizations without at the same time being able to influence their work.

Despite these developments, the institutional structure of new international relations had been rather loose and embryonic until the starkest violent images flew from Bosnia to the western capitals and prompted the international political fora to establish formal vessels whereby international law and the values of the "international community" would be directly imposed upon the countries that were at odds with those values. The massacre in Srebrenica in August 1995, when Bosnian Serbian troops attacked a UN-proclaimed Muslim "safe haven", guarded by Dutch UN peacekeepers, and murdered thousands of people in an "ethnic cleansing" policy of conquering a maximum slice of Bosnia-Herzegovina, triggered the final establishment of a firm rule of international law — it so seemed until March 1999, when the illusion was finally shattered. The ICTY, which was established by UN Security Council resolution no. 808 of 22 February 1993, initially served no apparent deterrent purpose. After the Srebrenica massacre, however, the President of ICTY, Judge Antonio Casseze, and the Cheef Prosecutor, Richard Goldstone, started an active policy of prosecutions by raising criminal indictments against the top political and military brass of the Bosnian Serbian Republic and Army, most notably Radovan Karadžić, the President of the Serbian Republic, and Ratko Mladić, chief general of the Bosnian Serbian Army, along with a number of other members of the Bosnian Serbian state establishment.[1]

The Tribunal was established with the purpose of deterring further aggression and transgressions of human rights, the international humanitarian law, and particularly the 1948 Geneva Convention on Genocide. Its goal was to represent the ultimate instrument of international law in meting out and enforcing international justice, as well as the ultimate instrument of the "international community's" *diplomacy* aimed at preventing the uncontrolled use of violence in the settlement of regional disputes.

The factual background of this latter intention was to be found in the fact that the security constellation in Europe in the post-Cold War era had been marked by security threats predominantly emanating from protracted low intensity ethnic, religious and territorial disputes. These were closely connected with the trend of state disintegration and political fragmentation in eastern Europe. The disintegration of institutions and control mechanisms in the region that arose from decreasing powers of the states after the fall of communism, caused the regional rivalries to be addressed by violent, rather than institutional and diplomatic means. This violence was marked by a *low availability of resources* (resulting in the predominant use of small weapons) and a *relative equality in strength* between the warring parties, resulting in the protraction of conflicts and sustained institutional, infrastructural and political devastation of the afflicted countries. The international organizations, that is, their most influential members, faced threats to their regional interests that they could seek to address in two possible ways:

(1) By using bare military force, which was an extremely economically expensive, and both politically and strategically risky option, or
(2) By using diplomatic techniques, which was an ideal, low-cost and clear, but often frustrating and time-consuming method.

Until NATO's military intervention over Kosovo in 1999, at least in Europe, the "international community" had chosen a combination of the two, where the insistence on the application of international law and responsibility to it had been seen as the main pillar of international diplomacy. After the Kosovo conflict, these principles appear somewhat more diluted, because for the first time in Europe since the Second World War a military alliance has conducted cross-boundary bombings without a broad international mandate conveyed by the UN Security Council.

While force has been applied to enforce some of the indictments raised before the Tribunal, so far the ICTY has primarily been seen as a judicial and — no less — diplomatic tool that has been aimed both to enforce justice, and convey a message containing the values of the new world order that was created after the Cold War. The image of ICTY, in important respects, has been the image of the great powers that have led the "international community". An impartiality, consistency and courage in prosecuting all violations of international humanitarian law in the territories of the former Yugoslavia since 1991 are the qualities capable of lending sufficient credibility to both the ICTY and those countries that principally stand behind it, in order for the ICTY's mission to be fully feasible.

In some cases, obviously, diplomacy alone cannot achieve extraditions and effect a sufficient degree of cooperation by the countries concerned, and in such situations force must be applied. However, the application of force in situations where diplomacy has not been given a proper chance, or the application of excessive force, or the use of force in other areas and contexts of international relations, contrary to international law and the established rules of contemporary international relations, may damage the esteem of the ICTY in the region. This may also reduce the degree of compliance with ICTY acts. An example of this danger is the strong national homogenization that has started in Serbia after the NATO bombings, which might mean that the state could become even more closed for cooperation with the ICTY in the future.

Multilateralism in the operation of the Tribunal

One of the main principles of the post-Cold War international relations has been multilateralism in decision-making. Bilateral relations are increasingly giving way to multilateral negotiations under the legitimization umbrella of large international organizations. The principle of multilateralism was upheld in the act of establishment of the ICTY. However, this has not been sufficient. For multilateralism to be thoroughly upheld, multilateral decision-making must be present throughout the operation of the ICTY. A consultative process needs to continually unfold under the Tribunal's roof, where all members of the United Nations would have a place at the table to voice their concerns and suggestions. All UN members, not just the most powerful ones, would have to be able to comment on the prosecution, trial procedure and execution of sanctions in whichever way they might deem appropriate.

While the general principle that countries should abide by the Tribunal's decisions has hardly been in doubt, the transparency of the Tribunal's work and the multilateral nature of its mechanisms and decisions has not been particularly clear. Only a few countries have maintained an active role in supporting the Tribunal and managing the control of its work, while those most concerned, namely the states of the former Yugoslavia, have appeared marginalized and absent from decision-making in The Hague. This has generated the impression that these countries were in effect being subjected to trial, rather than the suspected war criminals in them. The dominant and aggressive role of the US with its own, easily discernible agenda, has not helped the impression of multilateral democracy driving the Tribunal's role in these critical times.

The Tribunal's ability to mobilize international cooperation

One of the key roles of the ICTY has been to help create conditions whereby national reconciliation would be possible and likely, and maximize the potential for the establishment of cooperative links between the countries of the former Yugoslavia and leading members of the international community. Some functional cooperation has, of course, been an unavoidable result of the cessation of hostilities and normalization of production and trade in the region. Yet, war traumas are bound to remain extremely vivid in the consciousness of the population and an impartial, fair meting out of international justice is a key instrument for the facilitation of a faster healing process.

The Tribunal could have facilitated the catharsis of vengeful feelings and grief among the wounded nations of the former Yugoslavia if it had acted as a *filter of messages* between the communities formerly at war with each other. The theoretically imagined "field" of communication between the communities that had participated in mutual warfare was full of destructive messages or "waves" of distrust, animosity, insecurity and fear. This communication field was hardly an appropriate conduit for the achievement of stability and lasting reconciliation. It was polluted by an enormous amount of negative energy. This negative energy, theoretically, constituted regional instability.

The Tribunal's potential reconciliatory role here could be conceived as a filter between the communities inflicted by mutual warfare, ethnic and territorial conflicts. To be effective, the filter would have had to be of high absorption capacity and have a proper discriminative texture, so that it took out *only* the right messages or pollutants, and *all or most of* those pollutants. The Tribunal's substantive correctness and its efficiency in the execution of its mission were inseparable criteria for the evaluation of its work. Failures in either aspect have compromised the Tribunal's credibility and its effectiveness as both a judicial and a diplomatic tool in its reconciliation-building capacity.

One of the major setbacks in the history of the ICTY has been its lack of power to enforce arrest warrants and its subdued position to the political considerations of the great powers. This was the same setback that applied to any international organization when its proclaimed goals and methods of operation differed greatly from the real circumstances and priorities of its work. The ICTY was widely seen as a foreign policy instrument of the great powers for exerting pressure on Balkan countries, in line with their Balkan policy goals, rather than as a diplomatic instrument of the international community as a whole, whose purpose was to deflect destruction and/or perpetuation of violence in the region. The ICTY was thus not seen as being designed to provide an impartial judicial judgement of deeds, rather than persons and nations, which is the key role for any court. It was not seen as an international instrument for the re-establishment of values and the encouragement of mutual trust. This prevented the ICTY from playing an effective and credible role in international relations in the region. The filter appeared to have a wrong texture, the messages and particles that were stopped in it did not seem to be the right and only the right ones, and the filter seemed to be a low-absorption one, because political concerns of the great powers caused many who should clearly have been on the list of the ICTY to get away with their crimes. Political leaders responsible for violations of international humanitarian law remained largely uncharged, or at large. As long as this remained the case, the ICTY could not play a meaningful role in facilitating regional reconciliation, and it had to lag back in relation to the *Realpolitik* of the great powers.

A perspective on the future development of international war crimes tribunals

At the end of the 20th century, many would argue that the ICTY stands largely as a failure, but also as an important landmark. Many failures in history have played a navigating role in the subsequent development of institutions, practices and cultures that have eventually helped address burning issues of human relations. So it has been in politics, just like in any other area of human relations.

For the prospects of creation of a proper international war crimes court, or a reform of the ICTY, several prerequisites are essential. First, this includes the creation of a particular criminology for international war crimes tribunals, including the conceptual and procedural specifications necessary for the effective operation of such courts. Secondly, the building of an appropriate codex of international relations that would set a feasible context for such courts in their diplomatic and reconciliation-building mission is required. Finally, for international criminal tribunals for war crimes to be feasible, the shortcomings of the ICTY, the objections and answers to those objections regarding the legitimacy and impartiality of it, would need to be explored and translated into a set of specific policy recommendations for the future.

It could be argued that international war crimes tribunals have a future that is inextricably linked with their capacity to serve as effective diplomatic tools. Conversely, once they fail to abide by the principles of diplomacy, they are doomed. In this, they are unlike the national criminal courts. I hope that the forthcoming chapters will elucidate this point sufficiently.

Note

1 Notably enough, the initial indictments were brought forward almost exclusively against Serbs, which has harmed the Tribunal's credibility — see Fatić, A., "The need for a politically balanced work of The Hague International War Crimes Tribunal", *Review of International Affairs*, vol. XLVII, no. 1044, 1996, pp. 8–11.

2 The Nature of the Peace in the Former Yugoslavia: Heroes and Criminals — How to Distinguish Them?

Many people who have taken active part in the Yugoslav civil wars are perceived as national heroes, and an equal many are seen as villains by the international public. For sure, those who have committed gross violations of international humanitarian law should be taken to court. Yet, the criminals need to be identified and prosecuted consistently and on an equal footing, independently of what nation and what part of the world they come from.

The UN Security Council Resolution no. 808 established the jurisdiction of ICTY to try all those accused of violations of international humanitarian law in the territories of the former Yugoslavia as of 1 January 1993. This meant that all those actors present in the former Yugoslav territories since 1993 onwards were potentially liable under this provision, not only the local Yugoslav actors by origin.[1]

The crimes in Bosnia were recently rather well documented and, provided that a proper degree of impartiality and procedural efficiency by the Tribunal could be secured, it could be expected that all or most of those accused would eventually be tried. It was far less clear whether the Tribunal was going to institute any kind of responsibility for those from the ranks of the "international community", whose actions, willful and unwillful, have precipitated humanitarian disasters and war crimes. It was also totally unclear, and it remains unclear, whether the political leaders of the western powers would be brought to answer for their actions that had resulted in bloodshed and murder. People who, by their action or inaction, had contributed to the killings in Vukovar, Srebrenica, Skelane, Serbian Krajina, during the Croatian "Storm" operation, and elsewhere in the region actually taking place, were still at large in 1999. High UN officials whose action or inaction has cost the lives of thousands merely moved on to new high-ranking posts without having to suffer any consequences of their policies in Bosnia and Croatia.

Another issue concerns the protégé local politicians, primarily from the Muslim camp. Despite evidence that Muslim high ranking officials have been involved in war crimes, even that they have staged mass killings of their own to blame the other side (the Markale I and Markale II incidents in Sarajevo), not one Muslim leader has been charged. There was obviously a pragmatic reason for this from the point of view of the western powers — the political leaders whom they knew were easier for them to deal with politically than would be the political leaders whom they would not know. The current political leaders were also the ones with whom the ongoing negotiations and those planned for the near future were or would be conducted. Alija Izetbegović, the President of Bosnia, and Franjo Tuđman, the President of Croatia, support the current NATO expansion operations in Europe and are therefore needed by the West. Removing or antagonizing a negotiation partner would have obviously threatened the interests involved in the negotiations. Finally, if the political leaders were openly charged, their apprehension would become much more difficult. Failure to apprehend them, if they had been openly charged, could have effectively embarrassed the western powers, reduced their credibility, and impact severely on their leadership.

A particular problem with indicting leaders is that political leaders in southeastern Europe, and certainly those in the territories of the former Yugoslavia, enjoy considerable support in their communities. In some cases, this support may be a result of manipulation and misrepresentation of their actions and policies through state-controlled media, but political support nevertheless it is, and it has to be taken seriously in any strategies of bringing forward criminal indictments by ICTY.

A proper clarification of the issue of responsibility requires a distinction between legitimate and illegitimate military and political goals, allowed and disallowed means to be employed in the pursuit of these goals, the degree of foreseeability of the consequences of one's political decisions, and relevant elements of the circumstantial constellations of events, both locally and internationally. These four groups of considerations will be discussed here in some detail.

How to distinguish between legitimate and illegitimate military and political goals?

The main subject of ICTY is internal conflict. This type of conflict has been the most pronounced threat to regional peace and stability so far. The scope of the question here thus lies within the scope of the military and political goals that play a key part in internal violent conflicts.

Most of the relevant aspirations that tend to drive violent campaigns in internal conflicts were present in the Yugoslav civil wars 1991–9. My definition of the Yugoslav civil conflict contains two important conceptual differences from those most widespread in literature and among analysts. First, I speak of the Yugoslav civil wars in plural, because they were separate, although mutually closely related processes. They were *civil* wars in the former Yugoslav republics, not only civil wars of the former Yugoslavia (Socialist Federative Republic of Yugoslavia — SFRY) as a whole. The argument for the latter usually derives from the fact that the wars had erupted *before* the formal international recognition of the seceding republics as separate countries was granted, but in this case one would have to refer to these conflicts as to a single war, civil war of the former Yugoslavia. The same conflicts, then, would have to be referred to otherwise when discussing the period *after* the formal international recognition of Croatia and Bosnia-Herzegovina. This would cause unnecessary conceptual confusion, because the nature of the conflicts did not change after the recognition. My reason for defining the conflicts in the former Yugoslavia as civil wars is the following: What was at stake was a conflict between ethnic populations in the states (formerly constituent republics of SFRY, which then also had important attributes of statehood — their own parliaments, governments, judiciary, etc.) within the former Yugoslavia. These conflicts were driven by a desire for national emancipation and self-determination, regardless of the current landscape of national borders, which all populations felt as being at odds with their sense of nationhood and the pertaining sense of statehood. Slovenes, "Bosniaks" and Croats in the 1991–5 phase of the wars felt that the common Yugoslav borders no longer suited their sense of nationhood and statehood, so they initiated secessionist civil wars against SFRY. At the same time, Serbian communities in Bosnia and Herzegovina and Croatia felt the same about the borders of these two states, so they initiated civil wars against them. The involvement of the Yugoslav People's Army and later the Croatian Army in Bosnia contained legal elements of invasion, but they still did not change the nature of the conflicts themselves, which were civil.

Secondly, I speak of the Yugoslav civil wars 1991–9. The first phase of the wars was finished by the Dayton Peace Accords in 1995, but almost immediately the Kosovo conflict escalated along the same issues that had burned through the texture of the northern and central parts of the former Yugoslav society. In 1999, the Kosovo conflict became a fully-fledged civil war, and at the same time this is when the Yugoslav civil wars ended with the involvement of NATO on the side of the rebel Kosovo Liberation Army. This involvement opened a new chapter in the history of European warfare, thus ending the sequence of wars in the former Yugoslavia that could be characterized as civil. To be sure, many would agree that NATO's bombing over Kosovo was not merely an *arbitrary* act of aggression — it had a political rationale. However, it was an extreme policy, whose consequences have included considerable human casualties and unpredictable political dangers for the region, particularly for the civilians of FRY.

The break-up of the former Yugoslavia was driven by a conflict between two tendencies. The *first* was the national emancipation drive, triggered by the communist elites in the secessionist former republics. When the beginning of the central European transitions posed a threat to their ideological power-base they quickly resorted to encouraging a process of reassertion of ethnic identities and a quest of nation-statehood in the face of the remnants of the oppressive communist structures that they themselves had helped create and maintain. The *second* tendency was a desire of the federal government to preserve a level of centralism in decision-making. This tendency was strongly opposed by all of the constituent republics. In 1990, new Yugoslav federal elections were still possible. SFRY was the most economically prosperous eastern European country. The beginning of 1990 could see the former Yugoslavia off to a very fast and successful journey of joining the European integration tendencies and sealing the constructive, in fact rather spectacular, results of economic and societal reforms introduced by the federal government. But this line of developments did not suit the national elites in the republics, as the success of the reforms would have made them obsolete. They thus embarked upon a series of policies aimed to destroy the financial and economic stability and the country's security.

The national leaderships of the republics proceeded to break into the federal monetary system by printing money in their own mints, directly defying orders issued by the federal government. This caused the entire monetary system to enter into a state of chaos, the inflation reaching previously unprecedented levels, and the disintegrative tendencies among the Yugoslav republics starting to boil rapidly. The Slovenian Government started the break-up of SFRY by declaring independence, soon to be followed by Croatia, Bosnia-Herzegovina and Macedonia. The republics of Serbia and Montenegro remained together. Montenegro held a referendum, but its citizens decided to stay in Yugoslavia. The remaining federation of the two republics was renamed Federal Republic of Yugoslavia (FRY).

Simultaneously, Serbian minorities (quite substantial in numbers) in Bosnia and Croatia sought independence from those states and a right to remain in FRY. Serbs, who had been constitutionally defined as "a constituent nation" of SFRY, had suddenly become a national minority in the newly formed states of Croatia and Bosnia. They staged an uprising and managed to capture much of the territories of Croatia and Bosnia. Subsequently they declared their own states within those two countries, namely "Republika Srpska Krajina" and "Republika Srpska", respectively. Croatia and Bosnia, meanwhile, formed their own armies and engaged in a civil war against the two newly formed entities on their territories. In the course of the war, Croats formed a "Republika Herceg-Bosna" on the Bosnian territory, and another civil war erupted between Croats and "Bosniaks" (Bosnian Muslims) in Bosnia and Herzegovina. The linguistic acrobatics that have accompanied the progressive international recognition of new states and new nations in the territory of the former Yugoslavia have been stunning. So the Bosnian Muslims are now neither "Bosnian Muslims", nor "Bosnians" (for the latter include all citizens of Bosnia — Serbs and Croats, as well as Muslims) — they are now called "Bosniaks". Similarly in 1999, Kosovo Albanians are no longer "Kosovo Albanians", or citizens of Kosovo — they are now "Kosovars" — a term that is intended to somehow distinguish Kosovo Albanians from the other ethnic groups among Kosovo's citizens.

When these developments are closer analyzed, at least two levels of political goals become apparent. First, the goals of the former communist elites of the separatist former Yugoslav republics at the beginning of the state disintegration, and secondly, the goals of the national elites and leaders once the wars had started. Within the second set of goals, a distinction should be made between strictly *political*, and *military* aims and adopted strategies.

The goals of the former communist elites in the separatist republics

When SFRY started to disintegrate in late 1990 and 1991, there was no overwhelming hatred between its constituent nations and national minorities, as was often suggested. This was a fairly prosperous country with some understandable mutual animosities, dating back to the Second World War, but these were by no means glaring, and were certainly not a major political and security threat. They were no more pronounced than similar animosities in other countries of the region.

SFRY had ruthless communist state elites in the republics. The crushing of communist ideology in central and eastern Europe as of late 1980s confronted the ruling establishments with a prospect of losing their grip on power lest they found another ideology that was equally capable of quickly mobilizing public consensus and obedience. With an unmistakable zeal, they all turned to nationalism as the obvious choice. This turn to national chauvinism was particularly obvious and direct in Croatia, where the entire iconography and context of state ideology simply reverted to the times of the Second World War and the so-called "Independent State of Croatia" ("Nezavisna država Hrvatska"), when hundreds of thousands of Serbs, Jews and Roma were murdered in the concentration camps of the Nazi puppet state.

The exploitation of nationalism in the former Yugoslavia had a particularly brutal form — it included engagement in massacres, "ethnic cleansing", and genocide in Bosnia and Herzegovina. The political goal behind this was to generate a maximum degree of homogeneity under nationalist ideologies, and thus secure a rule based on political extremism. This meant generating antagonisms within the population, and developing a particular skill and mechanisms for channeling public disenchantment and dissatisfaction into those antagonisms, rather than allowing them to erupt as a desire to confront the government. Thus poverty, diplomatic and political isolation and a lack of prospects of personal and societal prosperity were successfully blamed on other nations, on the common federal state, or on neighbors from another ethnic group. The communist leaderships of all separatist former Yugoslav republics were masters of the *technology of power*. At the end of the second millennium, all of them are still in power, now as nationalist and national-emancipation workers, in all the separatist former Yugoslav states.

The most successful of the separatist manipulators and ethnic cleansers were the Croatian authorities, who not only committed gross violations of human rights against Serbs, Muslims and others, but also managed to ethnically cleanse as many as 400,000 Serbs from their homeland in the region of Krajina, in 1995. In this, they were actively assisted, equipped and encouraged by the US and Germany. After the successful conclusion of the "Flash" ("Bljesak") and "Storm" ("Oluja") ethnic cleansing operations, marked by a thorough "scorched earth" policy of murder, Croatia received no international condemnation and was never placed under any kind of economic sanctions.

The technology of power, of course, is not the same as good governance, and systematic failures in governance were offset by the use of advanced technologies of power in the generation of public support for the governments. Naturally, these techniques did not involve addressing the real needs of the population, including the need for a lasting security and economic prosperity. Neither of the populations of the republics enjoys any major improvement in security or economic progress today. One of them, Macedonia, is actually on the verge of a complete economic and security collapse and is the next flashpoint of internal warfare in the region.

The political goal of using diversions as the main technology of power to generate public support has been pursued to the extent of causing, and engaging in, civil wars and wartime atrocities. This compensated for the leaderships' incapacity for the multicultural and multiethnic management of a civil society. Franjo Tudman, the Croatian President, is known to have repeatedly claimed that he was satisfied to have entered history as the man who gave Croatia (and he used the phrase "The Independent State of Croatia" — not at all accidentally) its independence. That this was a militarist state built on the blood of southern Slavs, first of all the Serbs, and on the worst European traditions associated with Nazism, a state that had been made possible only by genocide and a removal of over 10% of its population, did not seem to matter.

All political elites of the Yugoslav republics were guilty of this abuse of political power. The Macedonian leadership is somewhat of an exception, because it was the only one that had neither provoked a civil war on its soil, nor participated in one on the soil of a neighboring state.

This pursuit of technologies of power to the extent of causing warfare and massive bloodletting was and remains a grossly *illegitimate political goal*. It is hard to conceptualize an effective way of sanctioning these actions, but it is clear that they belong to the prime substance the ICTY ought to be dealing with. Political leaders need to be made responsible for the consequences of their actions personally, and this is what the ICTY and the "international community" have failed to do so far.

Again, the most notorious proof of this failure has been the failure of the ICTY to indict Franjo Tuđman and his associates for the scorched earth policy in Krajina in 1995. In an article published that year, Cedric Thornberry, a human rights functionary in the UN, argued persuasively that this policy constituted a criminal campaign, and questioned the ability of ICTY to survive lest it starts indicting the top perpetrators of such actions. The "Flash" and "Storm" operations must have been ordered directly by Tuđman. They were actions that constituted a carefully planned and ruthlessly precisely executed mass murder of civilians, and as such represented a perfect examples of straightforward responsibility which had to bring Tuđman and his aides to The Hague. This concerns all other political leaders in the former Yugoslavia who remain uncharged at present, and who have designed policies of ethnic cleansing and mass destruction.

Instead of being allowed to present themselves to their citizenry as *heroes* of national emancipation, the political leaders who engage in the pursuit of atrocious policies, such as Tuđman, must be clearly and unequivocally condemned as *criminals*. The confusion between the two does not stem only from the mistakes *citizens* make in their judgement of their political elites — the citizens are subject to manipulation through the technologies of power and dominance, stories, half-stories, lies and half-truths, biased media and state repression. The confusion between heroes and criminals, on the contrary, is as much spurred and caused by the complacent "international community", which is too often too happy to successfully conclude a cease-fire and publicly shake hands of those who, by their pursuit of illegitimate political goals, have caused the wars in the first place.

By contrast, the pursuit of legitimate political goals in transitional circumstances involves a rigorous pursuit of economic stability first of all, integration into regional trade and cooperation projects, calming down of internal tensions, and soothing of ethnic divisions, with a view of securing the much needed continuity of development and a resulting growth in the transparency of all societal processes and activities.

No country in Europe is entirely immune to, or unaffected by, ethnic divisions, but many have moved on in spite of serious ethnic problems, even open conflicts, and are working on solving those through economic development and a quest for mutually acceptable compromise solutions. This has largely been possible due to an atmosphere of political moderation fostered by international organizations, predominantly the EU.

The transparent technology of power, which makes possible objective assessments of the government's performance, is a legitimate political strategy. The *divertive* technology of power, which obscures the government's systematic developmental policy failures, while channeling societal energy into conflictual relations and engagements, resulting in human casualties, is an *illegitimate* political strategy and ought to be sanctionable as such. The notion of criminal responsibility before war crimes tribunals should primarily depict the guilt of those who pursue *divertive technologies of power*, the foreseeable results of which include civil and other violent conflicts and wars. The diachronic (backward in time) process of establishing criminal responsibility in such cases would be quite consistent with the accepted methods of raising indictments and progressively accumulating evidence. A technically developed definition of divertive technologies of power and fairly precise criteria of reasonable foreseeability of those technologies resulting in civil violence could be designed, and would suffice to establish legally acceptable criteria of individual culpability. If this were the case with the processes underway at the ICTY, none of the leaders who have led wars in the separatist former Yugoslav republics would any longer be in the position to generate policy in the Balkans today.

On another level, once civil conflicts have started, the interests of those directly entangled in them assume a somewhat different shape and cannot be judged too simply. The perspective of a political leader heading a community in peace, who steers it purposely into war, is different from the perspectives of those lower-level leaders and community members who find themselves and their communities at war. The priorities of the latter are specific and, to some extent, deserve special considerations. Some political and military goals, violent and conflictual, may yet be legitimate in such circumstances. This, of course, does not mean that the killing of civilians, plunder of property, burning and destruction of towns and villages, should be tolerated or allowed, but it means that the responsibility of those who commit crimes *in* civil wars should be judged only after those who are the most uncontroversially guilty *for* the wars are brought to answer for their deeds. If this hierarchy is not upheld in bringing forward indictments, the system of international justice for war crimes will remain highly ineffective and devoid of credibility. This is particularly the case when criminals from highly organized military formations are concerned. For example, if a war crime is committed by members of the relatively amorphous "Kosovo Liberation Army" (KLA), it is quite possible that the immediate perpetrators or their immediate superiors bear the brunt of primary responsibility. However, when a war crime committed by a NATO pilot by repeatedly bombing a passenger bus or train is concerned, then there is no doubt that the general in charge must be indicted first, because it is he who has ordered the commission of a war crime.

What happens in a war? First of all, special circumstances apply immediately. These include official declarations of a state of emergency, and then a state of war. In such situations, all systems in society switch over to an entirely different mode of operation. Orders are much more difficult to avoid, and formal political hierarchies cannot be circumvented. A considerable, often dramatic, national homogenization occurs. Court marshals are introduced for many matters that in peacetime would have received only meager attention from civilian courts. The enemy is systematically demonized in the media. Disobedience becomes a crime of national treachery, which can more often than not entail death as a consequence. People often act in rationally inexplicable manners. The most horrifying crimes may occur in civil wars, and those who commit them are certainly guilty of them where they could at least theoretically have done otherwise, but not as much and not as immediately as those who, in peacetime, had contemplated, planned and purposely created the wars or conditions that they could reasonably expect would lead to war.

Secondly, criteria of *collective rationality* are reduced at times of warfare. What one person or a human group may or may not do in particular circumstances depends on their judgement of the danger they are exposed to, their options and the information and values that are not only served to them, but most often "drummed into" them.

Thirdly and finally, in every civil war there is a peculiar mixture of heroes and criminals in every community, and often in every military and paramilitary unit. Many known criminals have taken part in the civil wars in the former Yugoslavia. Some of them acted as commanders in situations where their actions were perceived and presented by their governments as quite legitimate. "For the national interests", they looted, murdered *en masse* and burned down entire towns and settlements, taking with them, often forcing them to do the same, people who had no choice but to obey or die. Again, the source of legitimization of such actions and at the same time the vacuum of individual choices for many of those who *would have* done otherwise came from the top of the political elites.

In short, for those involved in a war, the scope of legitimate goals is in fact operatively determined by their political leadership, in close synergism with the military leadership, and the scope for disagreement and disobedience is drastically narrowed down or taken away completely. This generates serious problems for determining criminal responsibility *if the culpability of the political leadership has not been determined first.* In fact, I will argue, it makes it almost impossible to consistently assign blame and criminal responsibility to those involved in civil warfare without *first* charging and condemning the political leaders. Criminals among the troops do not appear as criminals until criminals among the political leaders are stripped of the robes of national heroes and openly depicted and prosecuted as criminals. For example, it is almost bizarre that the ICTY is currently trying Croatian General Tihomir Blaškić for crimes against Muslim civilians in the Lašva Valley in Bosnia, when his President, Franjo Tuđman, who had ordered these operations, has not been charged first. If the political leaders of the communities that entered into the disintegrative inferno in SFRY in 1991 had been brought to trial in time, the bloodshed in the second phase of the wars would have been avoided, because those who had caused one war would not have been able to cause another one within just a few years. The following discussions will make this claim somewhat more easily intelligible.

The goals of those waging wars on the ground in the former Yugoslavia

In the Yugoslav civil wars, the goals of those involved in the conflicts on the ground (and, let me repeat this, they were *not* autonomous agents but ones bound by the hierarchy of leadership and the most broadly accepted values in their communities) were three-fold:

First, their goal was to achieve military victory, which involved *practically all means available* to obtain arms, ammunition, support, food and information.

Secondly, their goal was to secure the territory inhabited by their community *and enlarge it as much as possible.*

Thirdly, the goal was to maximally destabilize the political and military leadership of the enemy community, cause confusion and fear in it, and capture the strategic segments of the country's industry, land and technology.

There are two elements in the above three goals that are potentially problematic from the point of view of legitimacy.

The use of all practically available means to achieve military victory, including the burning down of towns and villages, trading with the enemy, etc., is illegitimate, and it should be the goal of the ICTY to identify those actions that take place within the pursuit of the goal to achieve military victory that constitute violations of legality and legitimacy. The ICTY should have had the task to determine whether the perpetrators of wartime atrocities were acting voluntarily, rather than acting out of objective or subjective (command and coercion) necessity. These are very sensitive legal and practical questions and the brunt of the work of international war crimes tribunals should be aimed at disentangling them in each particular case. Wholesale attempts to use one case as the scheme for all others are very dangerous, in this context, and the ICTY has played with such ideas in its work so far.

The second goal, or, more precisely, the part of it envisaging an extension of the territory controlled by a nation or ethnic group is, generally speaking, illegitimate. Wars of territorial conquest are forbidden by international law, and should be appropriately and efficiently sanctioned.

However, what deserves some consideration here is that, in some cases, it is difficult to practically distinguish between defending one's own territory and encroaching on another's. Ethnic conflicts are marked by high stakes and extremely vicious fighting. This often results in battles that get spontaneously carried over from ones of territorial *defense* to those of territorial *conquest*. This is not a legal excuse or a mitigating factor in itself, but it should be taken into account in trying particular cases to make sure that all possibilities of unpremeditated and unplanned, even unintentional attack, resulting in temporary or lasting territorial conquest, are duly examined.

Closely related to territorial conquest or consolidation, in fact often *contained* in this goal, are policies of "ethnic cleansing and genocide". These policies deserve the most stringent treatment by the courts, again along the line of responsibility that *starts* with the policy makers and commanders and *ends* with immediate perpetrators and their voluntary collaborators. Again, if there is ethnic cleansing, it deserves to be tried, but tried by courts and in accordance with international law — not by military assaults and by overzealous politicians, which sometimes tends to be the case. The latter constitutes a violation of international law. It is also greatly counterproductive in any regional crisis situation. This is extremely important — trying the immediate perpetrators without first, or at least simultaneously, trying the policy makers and commanders will *not* achieve the purposes of deterring further violations of the international humanitarian law and those of national reconciliation.

Policies of ethnic cleansing and genocidal slaughter of entire populations are broad in scope, and they require a systematic perpetration of atrocities over extensive territory. For this to happen, the policies themselves are most often centralized and closely coordinated. They are usually ordered from the very top of the political and military hierarchy. The immediate perpetrators of those horrifying crimes are often special police, military and paramilitary units, who are directly responsible to the very top political and military leaders, rather than ordinary troops and civilians.

The capture of such perpetrators is feasible, and the tracing down of chains of command responsibility is manageable within reasonable time spans, within the normal dynamics of work of international war crimes tribunals. These prosecutions need to take place immediately after the minimum conditions are secured, and they must allocate a high priority to capturing and trying those who have designed policies of atrocities, followed by prosecutions of those responsible for the commission of particular crimes. This order of prosecutions is important if two purposes are to be achieved — first, conformity to the logic of criminal responsibility according to the hierarchy of guilt, and second, the conveyance of the right message to the populations torn apart by the war, namely the message that what was done was wrong and intolerable from the point of view of the international community *as a policy*, and that independent international courts are prepared to pursue and prosecute *all* those guilty, regardless of their position and influence. This, then, means that those *not* guilty will be left to re-establish communal and inter-communal bonds and normalize life in the region after the war.

To achieve the degree of consistency required by this logic, which would lead to ethnic reconciliation, a great deal of courage and international consensus is needed. Unfortunately, that degree of boldness and initiative entails power-political risks that most key governments in the world today are unprepared to face. For this reason, and this reason alone, international justice for war crimes is not prevailing, and the message of reconciliation fails to be delivered.

The third goal of those involved in internal ethnic feuding and warfare is entirely legitimate in wartime, as long as it is part of a strategy of winning the war that does not involve shelling cities, killing civilians and prisoners of war, destroying public and cultural institutions, and other common war crimes. Destabilizing a political regime through propaganda in wartime is a legitimate strategy of warfare, yet this strategy can take many forms and, even if not accompanied by a direct use of violence and commission of war crimes, it can incite others to commit such violence and is thus by no means a benign method of warfare.

The pursuit of all three main political and military goals potentially entails human casualties, loss of resources, confidence, destruction of settlements and national wealth, deterioration in human relations in the long term, etc. War is a terrible thing, and it should not be thought that terrible things in wars are always and only the result of what is commonly regarded as criminal acts. There is a thin line that separates "legitimate" from "illegitimate" horrors of wars, especially ethnic and territorial civil wars. The later horrors are perhaps, sometimes at least, greater than the former. Perhaps. That judgement is extremely hard to make, and it certainly does not have to be correct in every war and every situation. However, the distinction is not based on the degree of horror involved, but rather on "objective" criteria concerning the nature of the actions committed, the status of the victims, etc. It is important to uphold this distinction in order to at least try to protect those who do not have to be targeted in a war. It is at least equally important to distinguish the transparent and peaceful technologies of power from the divertive and war-mongering ones, in order to try and sanction those bearing the prime degree of criminal responsibility for wartime crimes.

Compromise solutions and abortive peace settlements

The above distinctions and directions for action are extremely demanding of the outside intervenors, and require a major capacity to absorb and withstand internal political pressures, as well as vision and resolve, competence and personnel, allies and a favorable international environment.[2] This is why the "international community" has failed to adopt these conceptual presuppositions of an effective intervention and has ended up pursuing a compromise strategy resulting in a potentially abortive peace settlement in Bosnia, and a complete failure to secure the rights of the victims in Croatia.

Compromises and abortive solutions in Bosnia

The peace in Bosnia was "produced" by NATO aircraft attacks on the Bosnian Serbian troops, allowing the Bosnian Croatian and Muslim forces on the ground to push back the Serbs so much that they eventually had to sign a peace agreement brokered by the US. The Dayton Agreement, an extremely complex document containing both military and civilian provisions, effectively established a protectorate over most of Bosnia and

Herzegovina, with top political (civilian) and military control being performed by agents of the international community, led by the US. This solution costs enormously and lasts a very long time. In order to be sustainable locally, it was complemented by major compromises, the gravest of which, for sure, has been the failure to bring to international justice those most responsible for the horrendous atrocities in Bosnia. Instead of focusing on impartial justice for all those guilty of war crimes, in Bosnia the "international community" appears to have instead focused on furthering its own political interests in the region by the enormous exercise of discretionary powers by its "High Representative" for Bosnia, Carlos Westendorp. Mr. Westendorp has so far exhibited a perception of himself and his office where he is allowed to hire and fire state presidents, dictate to the Serbian media what they will broadcast and what editorial policies to adopt, etc.[3] The problems and policy failures in Bosnia cannot be blamed on non-cooperation by the former Yugoslav states, as is often the ICTY's habit, because Bosnia is factually a protectorate ruled by NATO and representatives of the international organizations, who have already arrested and sent to The Hague scores of suspected low-level perpetrators of war crimes. Yet, these forces have not yet arrested any leaders, particularly those from the Croatian and Muslim "camps", although they are still in Bosnia.

Not one political and high military leader from the ranks of the Bosnian Muslims has been indicted so far, although their political and military goals definitely involved causing civil warfare and the ensuing massive violence. Of all the Croatian top brass, only one general, Tihomir Blaškić, has been indicted, even though Croatian official troops had fought on Bosnian soil on the side of the Bosnian Croats when Bosnia was an internationally recognized country. The policies of the ruling Croatian Democratic Union ("Hrvatska demokratska zajednica" — HDZ) were an almost perfect example of aggressive and manipulative war mongering. These compromises have enabled the international community to develop a working relationship with Croatia and the Bosnian-Croat Federation, but they have set back the credibility of international justice and prospects for national reconciliation in Bosnia tremendously. The pragmatism of the key players in the international community have been the main debilitating factors for international justice in this region.

Why is the Bosnian peace settlement treacherous?

Bosnian peace as of 1995 has been secured through an effective occupation of the Republic by foreign troops and taking over of the greatest political powers by the High Representative of the International Community, who plays a factual role of Governor of Bosnia. Under the gaze of the heavily armed international troops who can dismiss local army units, political leaders, and intervene in the political processes, naturally, there is little or no maneuvering room for a renewed fighting. However, this type of peace settlement is inherently abortive, because, given the above described compromises, the international presence does not serve to re-establish inter-communal trust, but merely to *impose* temporary peace. Once the international troops leave (if they do), it will be very difficult to predict local developments in Bosnia, given that old feuds still persist and issues that have led to war, or at least many of the important ones, remain unresolved. What will then guarantee that the settlement will hold?

In fact, the "international community" knows that the Bosnian peace settlement is abortive and, in cooperation with NATO, it is gradually relinquishing an increasing slice of the peace-making competencies in Bosnia to NATO troops, leaving the door open for a lasting NATO presence in Bosnia even after the UN Security Council is forced to end the mandate of the SFOR units under the UN banner.

This problem is generally associated with international interventions in civil warfare and humanitarian disasters. The interventions need to have a clear strategy behind, with a clear specification of not only the goals to be achieved, but also of the effects on the local situation after the troops have left. It is not a good strategy to take on all management responsibilities in a society that is little known to the intervenors, and that is torn asunder by ethnic warfare, because this "freezes" the process of building civic initiatives and practices, and enormously increases the likelihood of renewed warfare after the international troops leave.

The Bosnian peace settlement was concluded in a manner that was required by the circumstances. It was necessary to stop the killings. However, its implementation is being rather badly done, and it leaves the door open for renewed conflicts in the short-to-medium term.

Heroes and criminals

As far as the wars in Bosnia and Croatia are concerned, the "international community" has failed to appropriately distinguish between heroes and criminals. The compromises it has sought have left it largely devoid of credibility in the region, as it has continued to negotiate with many of those who should be brought before the ICTY. The leaders of the western powers have consistently acted in the easiest way available, and have on occasions glorified those who should be tried for violations of international humanitarian law. The reluctance or open refusal of those regional warlords to cooperate with the ICTY and surrender those of their subordinates who had been charged, but who could incriminate the war lords themselves, has been natural — it could be expected. The problem with this really was not how to make the regional leaders surrender others, but why not charge the leaders themselves openly. The practicalities of turning those who present themselves to their nations and/or ethnic communities as heroes and national emancipators into criminals are complex, and by no means unequivocal. The key to success is bringing about charges as early as possible and as consistently as possible. An international community that has tolerated notorious war criminals for years, as long as it was politically easier and safer to do so, will have little credibility in bringing up charges later on, when it is politically, instrumentally opportune for them to do so, especially if the political opportunism in bringing up the charges is obvious to the region's population.

For a public perception to be shaped, the *motives* or the appearance of motives of those who are trying to shape it are of utmost importance. *Sincerity*, or appearance of sincerity, is key to a people being able to sympathize or identify themselves with charges brought against one of their own.[4] The perception of sincerity is enhanced if international reproach, institutionalized in international charges being brought forward, is expressed immediately after the atrocities have been committed or immediately after they have become known.

The "international community" that has tolerated persons accused of war crimes and others for years after the first alleged relevant crimes had been committed can hardly be believed to be sincere when it levels charges years later, in a bid to preclude major political consequences resulting from its inadequate — to say the least — political handling of a Balkan crisis. An international war crimes tribunal can equally hardly be believed to be an independent judicial institution if it openly acts in political synergism with those governments, hiding indictments and announcing them at politically opportune times for those powers.

Apart from generating major feasibility problems for capturing and trying suspected war criminals, breaches of international law by the major powers also diminish the ability of the war crimes trials that are successfully conducted to effect a reconciliation and a venting away of accumulated animosities among the parties in conflict. Many war criminals enjoy a status of heroes in their communities, and with the passage of time without a decisive, consistent and sincere action by the ICTY and the international troops on the ground, it will be increasingly difficult to take that status away from them and effectively proclaim them what they are.

Towards a deontic justice for international war crimes tribunals

It has been mentioned that the relevant concept of justice for international war crimes tribunals is of a *deontic* type. *Deontic* justice is the definition and type of justice that is based on certain substantive moral principles that must be applied *regardless of their practical consequences*, for the sake of the moral values inherent in them. Deontic justice is usually discussed as the antipode of *consequentialist justice*, which discriminates between morally justified and unjustified actions on the basis of the actions' consequences. Theoretically speaking, a perfect model of deontic justice and deontic morality *per se* is Christian morality, which commands unconditional love and tolerance, regardless of their practical consequences. Another, substantively different kind of deontic morality, is the Old Testament type of retributive justice that commands the principle of "an eye for an eye, a tooth for a tooth", again regardless of practical consequences. A classic example of consequentialist morality in moral theory is the so-called "utilitarianism" that prescribes a moral principle based on acting in such a way, appropriate to given circumstances, that is most likely to lead to the greatest amount of *benefit* or *utility* in its final consequences.[5]

In the realm of international justice for war crimes, people stand accused of serious violations of human rights and the international humanitarian law, with major state interests lurking in the background. Allowing consequentialism into the picture of justice here would inevitably lead to the individual being subjected to a web of state interests in the international arena, and thus sacrificed, or — probably more rarely — privileged and excused from responsibility, according to political considerations and state interests that have little or nothing to do with one's actual actions and intentions, and thus with one's actual guilt and responsibility according to accepted moral standards. Such a practice would deeply offend the common sense of morality and individual rights, and would thus, in turn, erode even the practical pillars of feasibility and compliance whereupon the system of international justice is supposed to stand.

I have argued elsewhere that in a national system of criminal justice a consequentialism of preventative type is preferred. This consequentialism, crudely speaking, envisages a non-penal confinement, where confinement is absolutely necessary, until the amount of *trust* in the perpetrator by the community is sufficiently restored for his or her reintegration into the community). The main reasons for this system of consequentialism in national criminal justice are three:

(1) All theories of criminal justice invariably come down to prevention as a key, if not the only, purpose of criminal sanctions, and the empirical and theoretical evidence leaves a large room for serious doubt that punishments serve a sufficient — or significant at all — deterrent function to effect prevention, both general and special.[6] Non-penal measures aimed directly at prevention through a degree of incapacitation (confinement), most directly linked to the community's readiness to accept the offender back into their ranks, seem the most effective imaginable protection from the point of view of the community.

(2) All restorative measures (principally, the restorative confinement) are strictly non-penal and involve a maximum of rights and opportunities for the offender. In the circumstances, this seems the best imaginable system of protecting the human rights of offenders.

(3) The principal "bridge" between the community and the perpetrator remains open after the perpetrator's incarceration (which happens only where it is unavoidable from the point of view of the seriousness of the offence — this system only applies to *crimes*, not to infractions or actions sanctionable under civil law — incarceration therefore happens only in the present context of *criminal law*, in other words, where it would have been the likely outcome anyway, even in the conventional criminal justice systems of today). Namely, the theory is "driven" by the concept of trust, which is, supposedly, seriously damaged by the commission of a crime and which, if and when sufficiently re-established with the passage of time, enables

the offender's release back into the community. This is therefore a functionalist, consequentialist, strictly non-punitive theory, that is the conceptual grid upon which, in my opinion, future and more humane systems of justice can be built.[7]

When the restorative theory briefly outlined here is carefully considered, it becomes clear that its consequentialism is far more determined, narrower in scope, and its parameters far more controllable — thus also being far less morally risky — than would be the consequentialism of any theory of *international* justice for war crimes. Consequentialism in a system of national justice involves mainly the post-trial treatment of the offenders, and consequentialism in international justice, due to the looseness of its structures and procedures, potentially involves the leveling of charges, treatment of suspects and detainees, trial procedures *and* the post-trial treatment. The post-trial treatment, except for the potential lack of supervision, which is much more difficult than in national criminal justice systems, is *the least controversial* part of the process.[8]

Much more controversial and immensely more vulnerable to political instrumentalization are the leveling of charges and the selection of those to be charged, the choice of charges, and the trial procedure — especially the rules governing the admissibility of evidence and related issues. These aspects of justice, which simply do not enter the realm of consequentialism contained in the restorative theory, and which are, I would dare to say, far less controversial in a smaller and much more transparent national system that is primarily concerned with actual crime control, are immensely relevant in international relations. They may help shape the opinion of millions and, if instrumentalized for the achievement of political purposes at politically opportune moments, they could seriously threaten the respect for individual human rights of the accused, or conversely, lead to letting those guilty of grievous crimes "off the hook" of justice. This is why the international system of justice must remain deontic and subject to straightforward, clear and immediate criteria of common sense credibility, arising from the more traditional norms of deontic justice. The key here is the traditional deontic apportionment of guilt, namely that all and only those guilty of war crimes must be immediately (or as soon as possible) charged. Those responsible must be charged *according to the priority established by the order of responsibility*, which in the case of war crimes starts with top leaders. The descending ladder of guilt envisaged by such a criminology would encompass all perpetrators, but it would be reasonable to expect that the top commanders would end up in prison sooner than the soldiers who, under their orders, committed violations of the international humanitarian law.

Notes

1. Such jurisdiction has been confirmed on a political level by the UN Nigh Commissioner for Human Rights, Mrs. Mary Robinson, in a statement to the European Commission on 30 April 1999, quoting a letter from the ICTY Chief Prosecutor, Louise Arbour. Mrs. Robinson specified that the ICTY had the powers to examine possible violations of international humanitarian law in Kosovo by Serbian security forces, the Kosovo Liberation Army (KLA), *or NATO*.
2. A "favorable international environment" here means a stable and controllable situation in the world. These policies can hardly be applied if, for example, the intervening country or countries are involved in several wars or crises around the world, are facing major internal or financial problems, or have pressing and unresolved issues in international relations themselves.
3. One particular example was that Mr. Westendorp actually demanded that Serbian Radio broadcast Reuters' news, or else he would shut it down. This is a highly interesting concept of promotion of democracy.
4. The reason I talk about "sincerity or appearance of sincerity" and "motives or the appearance of motives" is that I am discussing the *practical* political context of bringing those guilty of war crimes to answer for their actions, and in the practical politics of today perceptions and appearances are what counts in determining public reactions, often regardless of realities. It goes without saying, of course, that for international justice to be a true justice, to be *morally justified*, the real motives should be right, namely charges should be brought up out of a sincere desire to fulfil moral justice and effect a true reconciliation between the peoples by assigning the blame for atrocities to those who are really guilty, thereby releasing from collective guilt those who are not guilty. Unfortunately, it seems that in contemporary international politics such sincerity is scarce, and that the major actors at the international scene are acting much more out of particular political interests of their ruling elites, than on the basis of any authentic moral motives. I argue here for a largely deontic conception of justice as appropriately belonging to the realm of jurisprudence for international war crimes tribunals. This deontic concept of justice is somewhat in conflict with the dominant trend of extreme *Realpolitik* in international relations.
5. Contrary to what is widely believed, utilitarianism is an extremely complicated and controversial moral doctrine, its controversies stemming

mainly from the relatively open question of its definition, namely the question of the nature of the "benefit" or "utility" sought. This category can range from financial benefit to joy or satisfaction, the latter being the case in "hedonistic utilitarianism". Various sub-types of utilitarianism have been formed depending on how the core value is defined — such as "trust-utilitarianism", "rights-utilitarianism", and even "norm-utilitarianism". The broader in scope utilitarianism gets, and the more distant its core value becomes from the most simple and immediate concepts of utility such as financial benefit or joy, the more complex and less methodologically sustainable the doctrine becomes, as it increasingly overlaps with other moral theories, including deontic ones. These other moral doctrines have the capacity to methodologically "cancel" the utilitarian theory when the overlap is sufficiently extensive.

6   General prevention entails that punishing an actual offender should also scare other potential offenders from actually offending — to put it in an extremely simple form. Special prevention entails that punishment deters the actual offender from re-offending in the future — a very dubious theory, strongly contested by the high rates of criminal recidivism in most countries that have subscribed to it over the centuries. It is important to note that the death penalty is totally absent from a restorative system of crime handling.

7   At the time of creation of this theory, I took special care to avoid calling it a theory of "justice", as justice in moral theory is most often associated with deontic theories. That is why I used "crime-handling" instead, to emphasize the practical nature of the theory, although at first sight it has a detached, "ivory-tower" sort of appearance. Today I would be less reluctant to use the term "justice", but that is quite inessential to the theory.

8   The difficulty in the supervision of the execution of the ICTY's sentences, for example, arises from the fact that sentences are served in the prison space contributed by UN member-countries, which range wildly in traditions, prison-conditions and political and cultural attitudes to the wars in the former Yugoslavia, as well as to the particular parties that have taken part in the war.

3 The Political Landscape of Peace in the Balkans

A lot of political dust has been raised over the past few years concerning the relationship between the political settlement of the civil war in Bosnia, reached on 1 November 1995 in Dayton and signed on 14 December 1995 in Paris, and the obligation, arising from international law, for all sides to cooperate with the ICTY.

The relationship between political settlements and international war crimes courts is crucial for the modern shape of international relations. Unlike the earlier attempts to enforce justice on the perpetrators of war crimes (Nuremberg and Tokyo), the ICTY seeks to punish those who have perpetrated war atrocities in a civil war, not in an inter-state one. Political, legal and various practical circumstances are somewhat different for international tribunals dealing with war crimes committed in a civil war from those pertaining to international tribunals trying the war crimes committed in an inter-state war. There is one crucial difference here, and it lies in a specific *political*, in addition to a judicial, requirement posed before an international court dealing with crimes committed in a civil war.

In most cases, the sides in conflict in a civil war remain within common state frontiers, and their co-existence in peace requires a far greater degree of mutual reassurance and reconciliation than is the case in the aftermath of an inter-state war, where populations remain divided by a state border. In the former case, the populations in conflict share an army, common institutions, and living space. The task of all international organizations that intervene in a crisis therefore must be not only to fulfil justice, but also to maximize the opportunities for cooperation, mutual reassurance, reconciliation and confidence building between the parties in conflict.

For all these reasons, the ICTY, if it is successful, could be an exemplary case for modern international war crimes tribunals. It is a court that has borne a crucial relationship with the document that had established peace in one of the worst military crises in Europe since the Second World War, namely the Dayton Peace Accords.

Much of what is said here applies very generally, to all war crimes courts and to most atrocities, both in civil and in inter-state wars. But the main context of these discussions is civil war and atrocities committed in it. Dayton symbolizes the most difficult type of political settlements in a contemporary civil war, and is thus representative of the most complicated intervention cases. Both the Dayton Accords and the ICTY are representative of the indigestible post-settlement situations after a modern civil war.

The relationship between the Dayton Accords and the ICTY illustrates the specific connection between the judicial and political aspects of international war crimes courts' work.

The events preceding the Dayton Peace Accords for Bosnia and Herzegovina

The first phase of the Yugoslav civil wars that started in 1991 was a violent variant of the collapse of communist regimes in eastern Europe. The nations that had formerly lived in peace and served a common army suddenly found themselves at each others' throats for a greater piece of land for their independent states. Most analysts found it difficult to explain this, and some resorted either to one-sided characterizations of one party's "irrational aggression", or to simplistic physical or virusological analogies (spontaneous "boiling over" or "ignition" of "long suppressed" ethnic hatred, "contagion" by a virus of national statehood, etc.).[1]

Very generally and briefly, in the initial years of the war (1991–2), by using a kind of "Blitz-Krieg", Serbian forces in Croatia and Bosnia captured around 30% and 70% of the two countries' territories, respectively. Already in 1994 and 1995 the Serbian armies were exhausted from continued warfare in which they were sometimes thinly spread and had to maintain control of relatively large areas with very small local populations left (mass waves of refugees had already left Bosnia by 1994–5).

At that time, a gradual change of war fortunes started. In May 1995 the Croat Army, aided and trained by the US and Germany, stormed the Serb-held region of Western Slavonia, which had been traditionally inhabited by Serbs for several centuries. The area was under UN protection and the Croat assault was a major breach of the internationally brokered cease-fire. As a result, as many as 500,000 Serbs were ethnically cleansed. The sad convoys of civilians, stretching along the "Fraternity and Unity" highway towards Serbia were stoned by columns of aggressive Croats and paramilitary troops, under the approving gaze of the Croatian Army. Croat combat aircraft bombed civilian convoys and killed refugees. The area was subsequently kept closed for days by the Croat authorities, while it was being "cleaned up". The UN organizations were not allowed access to the critical area until a possible introduction of international sanctions against Croatia, similar to those that were in force against Serbia and Montenegro at the time, was discussed by the Security Council.

By the "Storm" operation Croatia regained control of about 95% of its territory from before the disintegration of the SFRY. The "Storm" offensive also radically aggravated the strategic position of Bosnian Serbs, who thereby lost the Serbian state that had been in between Republika Srpska in Bosnia and the state of Croatia.[2]

The strategic position of Serbian forces further worsened when the Croatian Army and Bosnian government troops concluded an uneasy military alliance in July 1995, in the Croatian town of Split. The Fifth Corps of the Muslim Government's Army in Sarajevo broke the Serbian siege of the Muslim enclave of Bihać, a town of utmost strategic importance in Bosnia. During 1995, Bosnian Serbs suffered serious losses of territory in Western Bosnia. Gradually, the situation on the ground started to correspond to the 1994 proposal by the International Contact Group for Bosnia (USA, Russia, France, Great Britain and Germany). According to this proposal, initially rejected by Serbs, Bosnia-Herzegovina would consist of two states or federal units, whereby the Croatian-Muslim Federation would control 51% of the territory, and Bosnian Serbs 49%.

The "international community", on the other hand, which was suffering a huge crisis of credibility because of its failure to intervene in the crisis adequately, decided to act offensively against the Serbs in 1995.

After the Bosnian Serbian Army captured the UN-proclaimed "safe havens" of Žepa and Srebrenica and took hostage UN peace-keepers in May 1995 to protect itself against NATO bombing, the Contact Group decided at its London Conference of 21 July 1995 to send a well armed rapid intervention force to Bosnia to protect the peace-keepers and the safe havens. Secretary General of the UN transferred his decision-making authority on the engagement of NATO bombers to his military representative on the ground. From 30 August 1995, NATO attacked Serbian targets massively and thus assisted Croatian and Muslim troops in pushing the Serbian Army back on many fronts.[3] This was the first open show of partiality of the "international community" in the conflict.

The only true beneficiary of all these externally induced developments was Croatia. It ethnically "cleansed" Serbs from Western Slavonia and captured a considerable part of Bosnia. Bosnian Croats even formed their own "Republika Herceg-Bosna" within Bosnia, which they hoped would secede from Bosnia and join Croatia.

This new, detrimental situation for the Bosnian Serbian Army was combined with a new tactic employed by the international mediators. In August 1995, Bill Clinton sent to Bosnia his own team of negotiators. Unlike the Contact Group, which had proposed solutions that the sides in conflict had been able to accept or reject, American negotiators allowed all three sides to actively participate in the negotiation and fight for changes and amendments to any proposed solutions.[4] On the other hand, they threatened the Serbs by NATO air raids and by a possible lifting of the arms embargo for the Muslim side. Should the Muslim side have decided to abandon the negotiations, it would face a withdrawal of all UN troops and lifting of the arms embargo for all sides. Once again, the only side that was openly encouraged or at least not directly threatened by adverse international measures were the Croats.

These military developments set the stage for the conclusion of an American-brokered peace settlement. In the settlement, everybody had something to lose except the Croats. The Serbs were facing direct international military action to help the other two sides to defeat them. The Muslim side saw the peace agreement as a chance, perhaps the last one, to "make official" the largest territorial gains it had made since the war had started, otherwise it could be "swallowed" by its two more powerful enemies (Serbia and Croatia), if abandoned by the Americans and Western Europeans (Russians were tacitly supporting the Serbs, and the Germans more or less openly supported the Croats). The Croats had everything on their side: the right to forge a "special parallel relations" agreement with the Bosnian-Croat part of Bosnia (which they hoped would, in time, mean a *de facto* annexation of that part of Bosnia by Croatia); an "ethnically cleansed" territory of their own; finally, they had escaped international sanctions and the international stigmatization that Serbia had suffered.

In November 1995, the Dayton Accords were initialed, then signed in December 1995 in Paris. As one American diplomat in Greece suggested to me in 1996: "The Dayton Agreement was signed with the IFOR gun barrels pushing into the backs of the signatories." It was an agreement enforced by military force and by the "international community's" taking sides in the conflict openly. This was objectionable from a formal point of view of impartiality, but it undeniably stopped the killing and saved

Serbian, Croatian and Bosnian lives. The Dayton Agreement was a complex political document, designed to be the basis of a lasting civil war settlement. As such, its implementation and the feasibility of its particular provisions are open to very serious questioning.

The Dayton political landscape

Dayton initially established a twelve month long mandate for the International Implementation Force (IFOR) in Bosnia. It was clear from the outset that the international forces would be present in Bosnia for many years. In 1999, four years after Dayton, they are still there.

The military provisions of the Agreement entailed that the rival armies would be separated, partially disarmed, that IFOR missions and command chains would be clarified, etc. These military provisions were implemented more or less fully and in time by all sides. However, the most problematic, and the most important part, was and remains the so-called "civil part" of the Agreement.[5] The political settlement established by Dayton envisaged that Bosnia-Herzegovina would consist of two "entities" — Republika Srpska and the Croat-Bosnian Federation. These two entities would share the Bosnian territory on a 51%–49% basis, respectively. Both entities would have their own separate armies and police forces. They would have the right to form "special parallel connections" with Croatia and Serbia, respectively.[6] They would have a common central government and a collective, three-member Presidency. They would both have separate citizenship and the right to enter into agreements under international law with other states. Each entity would develop its own defense policy. The common institutions, apart from the Government (or the Council of Ministers) and Presidency include the Parliament, the Central Bank, and the Constitutional Court.[7]

This political arrangement posed the question of how long and how far the central authorities could keep the two entities together. Some influential commentators suggested that Bosnia would eventually have to split-up into two separate states.[8]

Annex 10 of the Dayton Peace Accords envisaged that the "Sides" would endeavor to "promote observance of human rights", facilitate the return of refugees and displaced persons to their homes, and other difficult tasks relating to the re-creation of a civil society in Bosnia.

Annex 10 envisaged the appointment of a High Representative of the International Community to coordinate and supervise the implementation of Annex 10. The High Representative was to play an extremely important role, because of the numerous competencies entrusted to him that ranged from coordinating the activities of the two sides to calling for coercive international intervention to force the sides to cooperate in the implementation of Dayton. It has not become entirely obvious just how sweeping the powers given to the High Representative were until Carlos Westendorp attempted to sack the elected President of Republika Srpska, Nikola Poplašen, in 1999.

The critical nature of the "civil" provisions of the Agreement

Generally, the civil part of the Dayton Peace Accords was aimed at establishing a civil society in Bosnia. Such a society presupposed a regeneration and revitalization of mutual confidence and ability to live together. People whose family members had been butchered by the family members of many of their neighbors, not for the first time, would find it difficult to continue living together under the same authorities. A foreign presence was seen as necessary for their mutual reassurance, but that presence, in order to be effective in generating reconciliation, would have to be maximally impartial, which was not the case.

Dayton was also aimed at helping to achieve the political stability necessary for societal revitalization. It did not convincingly resolve the questions arising from the three nations' quest for national state sovereignty — the division of Bosnia into two entities with three constitutive nations, while at the same time insisting on the preservation of its unity under extremely loose and powerless common institutions, with two independent armies, was a difficult solution to achieve. This was a strategic solution that could only hold if it was supported by an effective occupation by foreign troops, and that has been the case ever since the conclusion of Dayton. The whole situation did not provide sufficient conditions for a revitalization of civil society, informal community, and inter-communal bonds.

The status of refugees was a particularly pressing problem. Most of the people who had been expelled from their homes subsequently spent five or more years in their new "homes" and established community bonds and family arrangements that tied them in the long term to their new place of residence. They had nowhere to return, in most cases, because their homes had been torched, their neighbors had gone somewhere else or had been killed or maimed, and their memories were a torment to them. Despite all of that, the rhetoric of "return of refugees" became an excuse for the host governments in western Europe to get rid of the unwanted social burden, while at the same time creating even more sorrow in the ravaged Bosnian lands, by up-rooting again the people who had already been displaced, many of whom had small children who had started to go to school, and had sensed a new "home" environment around them. Such a "return of refugees" was yet another crime against humanity in Bosnia.

This proposition could be easily tested. There was never any shortage of politicians who would readily embrace the policy of "return of refugees" (at least of those of their own nationality). This applied both to those who had used to be war lords and were subsequently presenting themselves as "democrats", and to those "western democrats" who were expelling refugees for internal economic reasons, despite appeals not to do so by humanitarian organizations.

The status of refugees in many countries that had initially "generously accepted them" in large numbers remained unresolved for years. They had no right to work and therefore no basis for reasonable expectations of any life constancy and stability; they had no passports or were in the process of effectively losing those they had had, because they were unable to renew those documents once they expired. A large majority were unemployed and legally unemployable; their freedom of international travel was limited; they had no means to secure adequate legal protection; no right to own property or means to secure a stable and adequate accommodation — in other words, refugees remained at the mercy of their "host" governments literally every day.

Granting the refugees citizenship and the corresponding elementary civil rights was therefore imperative for their well-being and for the gradual quelling of the feelings of spatial, national, and emotional upset and revolt in these territories that had used to be killing fields until so recently. True, Dayton envisaged only *the right* of all displaced persons to return safely to their original place of residence *if they wished to do so*, but this was far too often interpreted by the host governments as the right to either expel refugees to where they had initially come from, or to deprive them of their civil rights and thus effectively force them to return.

The voice of refugees was not heard in international decision-making bodies. Yet, it was their experience of the war that told the accurate story about the most plausible ways to proceed in the direction of conflict-resolution and re-building of a civil society.

The connection with the ICTY

The establishment of the ICTY was driven by considerations arising from efforts to reach a political settlement to the crisis in the former Yugoslavia. While the atrocities committed in the war were the deciding factor for the actual establishment of the Tribunal, the historical context in which the war occurred was also important. Namely, when the fighting in Bosnia erupted, there was already talk of bringing those responsible for violations of the international humanitarian law to answer for their actions before an international court.

The idea itself went back to the immediate aftermath of the First World War. The then assembled "Commission on the Responsibility of the Authors of the War and on Enforcement of Penalties" proposed the establishment of a "high tribunal composed of judges drawn from many nations". Article 227 of the Treaty of Versailles included the provision for the establishment of an international tribunal, with five judges from the USA, Great Britain, France, Italy and Japan, to try Wilhelm II, the former Kaiser of Germany.

In 1920, the Advisory Committee of Jurists, formed by the Council of the League of Nations to prepare the proposal for a Permanent Court of International Justice, called for the establishment of a High Court of International Justice, which would also try all crimes that constituted breaches of international humanitarian or public law. The Assembly of the League of Nations rejected this proposal.

After a sequence of proposals, none of which had been implemented, the first international war crimes tribunals to be established were the Nuremberg Tribunal in 1945, and the Tokyo Tribunal in 1946, which were set up by the victorious Allies to try the war criminals from the ranks of Nazi Germany. As these two tribunals were designed exclusively for trying the perpetrators of war crimes from within the Nazi German Army and other allied formations, during the Second World War, once these trials were over, the Nuremberg and Tokuyo tribunals lost their legal basis.

In 1948, the international Genocide Convention was signed, whose Article 4 contained the provision that an international penal tribunal was to be established. In that same year, the UN General Assembly called upon the International Law Commission to examine the possibility and usefulness of setting up "a Criminal Chamber of the International Court of Justice". Although nothing came of these initiatives, in 1989, after the end of the Cold War, the UN General Assembly again called upon the

International Law Commission to discuss the possibility of establishing an international criminal court.[9]

The ICTY was established at the proposal of France, by the UN Security Council Resolution 808 (1993) of 22 February 1993. The sequence of events leading to the establishment of the Tribunal was as follows: first the idea was voiced to the two mediators for the former Yugoslavia, Lord Carrington and Cyrus Vance, by Robert Badinter, who at the time was President of the Arbitration Commission for the Former Yugoslavia. On 26 August 1992, at the London Conference on the Former Yugoslavia, German Foreign Minister, Klaus Kinkel, re-vamped the idea. He was supported by the French Minister Roland Dumas, and the proposal became one of the conclusions of the London Conference. A new series of proposals to the same effect came, by Kinkel (on 23 September 1992 before the UN General Assembly), Elie Wiesel (December 1992, to the US Secretary of State Lawrence Eagleburger), by Lawrence Eagleburger (statement to the Geneva International Conference on the Former Yugoslavia, on 16 December 1992), by Ronald Dumas (in a Declaration of 6 October 1992 on the occasion of the adoption of the UN Security Council resolution 708), by the Commission of Experts set up by the Security Council in 1992, and by the International Conference on the former Yugoslavia, on 30 January 1993.[10]

On 16 January 1993, Ronald Dumas appointed a Commission of Jurists to draft a statute of an *ad hoc* international tribunal for war crimes in the territory of the former Yugoslavia. This and other drafts were then used by the UN Secretary General in his drafting of the Statute of the International Criminal Tribunal for the former Yugoslavia.

The ICTY has been an attempt to resolve some of the critical issues that had remained after Dayton, primarily the issues of guilt, responsibility and reconciliation. One of the main tasks of the ICTY, when it was established in 1993, was to deter new atrocities. In this, it was unsuccessful. It was created *before* Dayton, and some of the most serious war crimes occurred while it was operational. This illustrates two main problems. First, many war crimes, as one could imagine, are committed by people who are, to say the least, highly irrational or psychopathic, and who do not count on ever having to actually answer for their actions. Second, the credibility of the international organizations that would reasonably be charged with bringing those accused of war crimes before the Tribunal was severely compromised. Very few perpetrators in Bosnia and Croatia even believed that they would face the court in The Hague. The first problem, connected with the irrationality of most serious crimes and the corresponding low preventative value of punishment, is, unfortunately, rather general, does not apply only to war crimes, and is probably insoluble by using penalties alone.[11] The second problem was avoidable.

Notes

1. See Brown, M.E. (ed.), *The international dimensions of internal conflict*, MIT Press, Cambridge, Mass., 1996, especially "Introduction", pp. 1–32, for a useful critique of such analogies.
2. Čalić, M–J., "Bosnia and Herzegovina after Dayton: Chances and risks for peace", *Review of International Affairs*, no. 1046–47, July–August 1996, pp. 13–7.
3. Ibid.
4. Ibid., p. 14.
5. The civil part envisages things such as return of refugees and displaced persons (Annex 7, articles I–II), cooperation of all sides with international organizations and international monitoring (Article III), repatriation assistance (Article IV), accounting for missing persons (Article V), granting a comprehensive amnesty to all apart from those suspected of having committed war crimes (Article VI), free movement of people within and between the two "entities" (Annex 4 — "Constitution of Bosnia and Herzegovina", Article II — "Human rights and fundamental freedoms" — paragraph 3, point (m) — "The right to liberty of movement and residence", also Article I, paragraph 4 — "Movement of goods, services, capital and persons"), *The Dayton Peace Accords*, as released by the US Department of State Foreign Affairs Network, Internet edition, http://dosfan.lib.uic.edu, Office of Public Communications, Bureau of Public Affairs, US Department of State.
6. There have been subsequent attempts, however, by the High Representative and major international intervenors, to stifle initiatives by Republika Srpska to forge a "special parallel connection" with Serbia.
7. *Constitution of Bosnia and Herzegovina* (Annex 4 of the Dayton Accords), Article V, paragraph 4 — "Council of Ministers"; Article V, paragraphs 1–3 — "Presidency"; Article IV; Article VII.
8. Henry Kissinger, for example. His comments have drawn criticism by the USA Administration.
9. "The path to The Hague: Selected documents on the origins of the International Criminal Tribunal for the Former Yugoslavia", internet edition, www.un.org/icty
10. Ibid.
11. This is a separate topic — see, for example, Fatić, A., "Psychopathy: Cognitive aspects and criminal responsibility", *The Criminologist*, vol. 21,

no. 2, 1997, pp. 64–75; also published as "Criminal responsibility and personality disorder", *Arhiv za pravne i društvene nauke* (*Archive of Law and Social Sciences*), vol. LIII, no. 2, 1997, pp. 279–90, especially Appendices 1 and 2 with diagrams representing *mens rea* responsibility and the types of "mental problems" constituting excuses from the so-called "full" culpability.

4 The ICTY's Aspirations, its Statute, and Some of the Legal Inconsistencies in its Establishment

The establishment of the ICTY was driven by a dual motive:

(1) By a desire to deter further killing and torture, along with putting a lid on the conquering aspirations of the sides in conflict, and
(2) By a frustration with the inability of international players to contain the war in the former Yugoslavia, and a corresponding desire to restore trust in the "international community".

Both aspirations remained unfulfilled. The killing continued after the establishment of the Tribunal, and in fact some of the worst atrocities occurred between the establishment of the Tribunal in 1993 and the conclusion of the Dayton Peace Accords in 1995. The Tribunal did not help the "international community" to regain its status as a credible power and intervenor, but rather lagged behind its other efforts. Only after the Dayton Peace Accords had been signed did the ICTY come back into the focus of peacekeeping efforts in the former Yugoslavia. The Tribunal's work, in fact, naturally followed political and military efforts. Such efforts could secure the conditions conducive to effectively bringing about cooperation by the sides involved in the conflict with the Tribunal. Without first securing the operational, military and political presuppositions for penalizing those accused of war crimes, the mere establishment of an international court for war crimes had no or little deterrent value for war criminals. Failure to fully realize this made it almost inevitable that, in the first few years of its operation, the Tribunal did not and could not play a successful role in preventing atrocities and criminal loss of life during the war, nor was it a successful political tool of the "international community" for either bringing the war to an end, or maintaining/restoring its own credibility. After the peace had been concluded and Dayton signed, the

Tribunal had one major role left to play: to bring the peoples torn apart by the war together again, by helping them to achieve a catharsis through clarifying the issue of guilt for wartime atrocities.

To achieve the aim of reconciliation and just allocation of guilt, the legality, impartiality and legitimacy of the Tribunal's work would have to be impeccable. The nations that were involved in the Yugoslav wars, first of all FR Yugoslavia, have questioned the legitimacy of the Tribunal on several grounds, largely by drawing parallels between it and the principles and practice of national criminal legislation and criminal justice systems.

The objections to the Tribunal

1. First, it has been objected, notably by the Yugoslav government, that the Tribunal was illegitimately established, because it was established by a Security Council resolution, rather than by a decision of the General Assembly of the UN. This objection is based on a parallel with national legal systems where courts can only be established and controlled by Parliament (the national equivalent of the UN General Assembly), and never by Government (the national equivalent of the UN Security Council).
2. The second most widespread objection is that the Tribunal's Statute is in conflict with the national constitutions of some of the countries of whom extradition of indicted war criminals might be asked (again notably FR Yugoslavia), because constitutional provisions forbid extradition of the country's nationals to other countries or international organizations.
3. The third objection is that the Tribunal is primarily designed as a political instrument intended to exercise pressure against one side (notably the Serbs) and lead to its lasting stigmatization and isolation, and only secondarily as a judicial instrument intended to enforce justice internationally. Arguments in support of this objection have mostly revolved around the perceived disproportion between the initial numbers of indictments brought up by the Tribunal against the Serbs as opposed to those against Muslims and Croats.
4. The fourth objection concerns the treatment of convicted war criminals. The Tribunal's Statute prescribes that all those convicted will serve prison terms in prisons of the UN member countries that voluntarily contribute prison space. It is argued that this severely

compromises the principle of equality of penal treatment, because some prisoners will be sent to relatively "civilized" western European prisons, while others will serve their terms in the prisons of Pakistan, Turkey, India, etc., where prison conditions are much more severe. Furthermore, since there is a religious element involved in the international judgement of the conflict in the former Yugoslavia, there is room for fear that those from the Serbian and Croatian sides who might be sent to prisons in Muslim countries might be killed or otherwise victimized, and vice versa.[1]

Commentary of the objections

The *first objection* has some plausibility if it is assumed that parallels between national and international organizations are relevant for assessing the legitimacy of the latter. It would have been ideal, in terms of the international consensus, if the Tribunal had been established by a decision of the UN General Assembly. Still, the Security Council is undoubtedly that part of the Organization where real powers are vested. The Security Council overseas and implements all UN decisions concerning peace and security matters.[2] This means that, even if the ICTY had been established by the UN General Assembly, the Security Council would still have been charged with implementing that decision and bringing those accused of war crimes to trial. This would, as it does now, involve pressure on the countries concerned, military, economic, and diplomatic, to extradite the accused and cooperate with the Tribunal. The source of that pressure would have been the Security Council, as it is now.

Because of their superior power-position in the UN compared to those of the other members of the General Assembly, the five permanent members of the Security Council (P5) would have been able to impose their will regarding the establishment of the ICTY on a large number of other General Assembly members. In other words, if one is realistic, one must conclude that it was probably inevitable that the *Security Council members, particularly the P5, would largely determine the modus operandi of the Tribunal.*

The point of this objection, raised by the Yugoslav government, is therefore not that the Tribunal would have acted in any different a way, had it been established by the General Assembly. Instead, the objection goes more to favor the assumption that, should it have been up to the General Assembly, the ICTY might *not* have been established in the first place.

The objection is materially dubious. Pressure from the most influential UN members, who make up the Security Council, would have swayed many of the General Assembly members who might have been opposed to the establishment of the Tribunal — and it is doubtful how many, if any, were really decisively opposed to it. Although it might have been theoretically more desirable had the ICTY been established by the UN General Assembly, the Security Council passed the resolution on the establishment of the Tribunal under *Chapter 7* of the UN Charter. All resolutions passed under Chapter 7 are obligatory for all UN members, which means that there was no strictly *legal* controversy in the way the Tribunal was established.[3] The first objection is therefore rather weak.

The *second objection* appears equally weak. While it is true that some national constitutions prohibit extradition of the country's nationals to a foreign or international court or authorities, Chapter 7 of the UN Charter *obligates* all members to cooperate with the UN and implement Security Council decisions. In addition, the Dayton Peace Accords envisage cooperation of all countries concerned with the international organizations, and this implies also with the ICTY. Finally, international agreements, conventions and obligations *take precedence* over national laws, and represent at the same time a part of the internal legislation of the signatories. This position concerning the applicability of international law when in conflict with a national legislation has been formulated in the law of the European Union as the so-called "Principle of Direct Applicability": Wherever a national law is in conflict with EU law or with the decisions of EU bodies, the EU law takes precedence and is applied *directly, regardless* of the national law. The same principle, at least theoretically, applies to international law in general. Many countries have built the direct applicability of international law into their constitutions. Yet, trampling the "national jurisdiction" by international law remains a problem in many parts of the world, and the debate on this matter is far from being over. The problem is therefore more practical, than legal or theoretical.

The *third objection* is the most politically interesting and controversial, for there is hardly any doubt that the ICTY is a source of much pressure on some Balkan governments. The pressure comes from two focal points, and is of two kinds.

First, it comes from the operational need to secure cooperation with the Tribunal by the countries harboring the accused. This type of pressure can hardly be avoided if justice is to be served and it only makes sense to ask about the most productive *modes* of pressure so as to both achieve cooperation in the most efficient way, and not at the same time inflict so deep wounds on national economies, psyche and political systems, to make the emergence or re-emergence of a legitimate society after the pressure period harder or impossible.

The second source of pressure comes from perceptions of the guilt of particular countries that have taken part in the Yugoslav wars so far. All three countries involved in the first phase of the conflict had their "patrons" in the Security Council or among other powerful members of the International Community. The Bosnian side's patron was the USA Administration, because of the perception amongst that administration that "Bosniaks" were the victims and losers in the war, and because of the US's perception and definition of the war as one of aggression against an independent state, rather than as a civil, internal conflict. The Croatian side's patron was widely seen in the newly re-united Germany, which was the most powerful political player in Europe. Apart from being widely criticized by its allies for having "pushed" them to prematurely recognize the independence of Slovenia and Croatia (this later logically led to the recognition of Bosnia-Herzegovina as well), although she is not a permanent Security Council member, Germany has exercised significant influence at times, which was sometimes interpreted as having been intended to protect Croatia and advance Germany's interests in the "international community" after the Cold War. Some of these perceptions were largely shared by some of the Croatian establishment. The question of Germany's role in the international involvement in the Yugoslav wars, and especially its perceived support for Croatia, is a complex issue. However, in analyzing the development of international relations in the former Yugoslavia, perceptions of the foreign countries' alignment in relation to particular actors in the war in the former Yugoslavia is of key importance. It may not be the case that any of the mentioned countries had any differentiated and developed policy of support for any specific country in the former Yugoslavia. Most of them declared so. But at the same time, they were perceived as having preferences and animosities in the war, and these perceptions are relevant to note here. It is interesting that at one point the Croatian television launched a song in German, performed by some of the best-known Croatian musicians, which was titled "Danke Deutschland!" ("Thanks to Germany"), to celebrate its independence and a resurgence/re-affirmation of Croatian nationalism as the official and predominant political current.

The Serbian side, traditionally, kept counting on its old ally Russia. Although a great power and a permanent member of the Security Council, and although it verbally advocated Serbian interests, Russia was eventually seen as a feeble ally for the Serbs.

To use an oversimplified pictorial metaphor, in the times of sociopolitical transition, Russia remains a giant on its knees. It is so economically and diplomatically dependent on its western partners, and it has so many of its own problems, including civil wars (Chechnya was the most drastic example), the position of its minorities outside its borders, its disarmament strategy and obligations, and many other critical areas of national policy, that Russia has never really been in any position to stand firmly behind the Serbs and fully protect them from concerted pressure and even military actions by her western partners, throughout the Yugoslav wars.

Russia is in a historical defensive position. It appears to be struggling to maintain the status of a superpower, which it has already lost. It seems that Serbs have had more practical support from their regional ally Greece, which subtly advocated their interests in the EU and equally subtly maintained some trade and diplomatic cooperation with Serbia during the EU and UN economic sanctions, than from Russia. Admittedly, the support expected of Russia was of a more dramatic nature than that expected of Greece — Russia was falsely and unrealistically expected in Serbia to block Security Council resolutions against the Serbs to the detriment of her own interests. She was even expected to protect Serbian troops militarily. While the Russian government was unable to go to such dramatic lengths to protect the Serbs in the first phase of the wars, it did maintain supplies of gas and oil to Serbia in Winter, especially after the lifting of the sanctions, and in spite of the large debt in unpaid fuel by Serbian petrol companies and Serbian government. Russia also persistently argued for a lifting of the sanctions against FR Yugoslavia, and on a number of occasions it even sought, on a verbal level at least, to deter military actions against Serbia itself. At one stage in the first phase of the war, when collective decision to act militarily against the Serbs was at the highest level in the Security Council, an option of bombing strategic supply routes and bridges in Serbia itself, which were strategically important for Bosnian Serbs, was seriously considered. It should not be forgotten that Russia opposed this option very strongly, and at one stage the Russian government threatened that it would deploy its fighter aircraft to Serbian airports to protect them from being targeted by NATO jets. In fact, from what was reported in the media, Russia could be considered to have saved Serbia itself from direct military assault by NATO at the peak of the conflict in neighboring Bosnia.

In this second sense, the political "pressure" exercised by and/or through the ICTY has been connected with the question of which side's patron was most in control of the Tribunal. It is probably correct to say that the US has been most in charge of The Hague court. So, perhaps the pressure, emanating from the first charges brought up before the Tribunal, was indeed aimed mostly against the Serbs, and later the Croats. For example, this concerns the charges brought up against Radovan Karadžić, former President of Republika Srpska and President of the ruling SDS — Srpska demokratska stranka (Serbian Democratic Party) and General Ratko Mladić, Commander of the Bosnian Serbian Army, for crimes committed in the UN-proclaimed "safe havens" of Srebrenica and Žepa, in August 1995.

Perhaps the war criminals from the Muslim camp have not been treated equally with the ones coming from the Serbian and Croatian camps so far. This is impossible to assess accurately, because of a lack of comprehensive information about the actual numbers of crimes committed by each side, and a lack of their precise chronology. If there is any pressure in this sense, it comes from the fact that only one of the three "patrons" has had a large input in the actual operation of the ICTY. The US is the greatest financier of the ICTY, its troops spearhead the international forces in Bosnia on whom the Tribunal ultimately depends for enforcing its decisions and eventually securing the arrest of the accused. The US is militarily the largest contributor to UN peace-keeping missions and the country with the most assets to contribute and the most economic and diplomatic influence world-wide. As such, it has the most pronounced opportunity to influence the ICTY. On one level, this is a natural consequence of one country's dominance in military, economic and diplomatic areas within any international organization. However, on another level, it is an *extremely dangerous* kind of pressure for the prospects of mutual reconciliation in the former Yugoslavia.[4]

The impartiality of the involved international players is critical for reconciliation and for the goal of preventing a continuation of hatred and grudges, and thus also of a new war in the near future. In this way, impartiality is a requirement at present for saving lives in the near future.

Of all the objections, this third one, in the sense of partiality of pressure based on selective protectionism, ought to be taken very seriously and examined to find out whether it is grounded in reality. If it is found to be well founded, then the ICTY might well be working to the detriment of prospects of a lasting peace, rather than to enhance these prospects. The importance of impartiality of any coercive or incentive-building international intervention in the immediate post-civil war/post-settlement period can hardly be overemphasized. The level of mutual confidence between the formerly confronted populations is so low in the post-settlement years that the international presence is required primarily for the prevention of a re-escalation of tensions, and for a gradual mutual reassurance. If the international actors, including the ICTY, are seen as in any way taking sides, the prospects of reconciliation in this troubled part of Europe could be buried, and a future moment of departure of the international troops (which will inevitably come) might mark the beginning of preparations for a new imaginary "final" — military solution.

The *fourth objection*, based on unequal conditions of imprisonment between various UN members, is also valid. The current statutory provision clearly rests on practical exigencies — the Tribunal has no independent prisons of its own in The Hague where all war criminals could serve long prison terms. It therefore has to depend on UN member countries to donate prison space. But this does not justify inequality of penal treatment, however grave the crimes of the convicted individuals. This problem needs to be solved by committing greater resources to equalizing the prison conditions for convicted war criminals from the former Yugoslavia, wherever they might be serving their sentences. There is much to be said about how this could be done, but it is a practical question that goes beyond the domain of this discussion. Two key words are sufficient here: *resources*, and UN *supervision* of all those imprisoned under sentences passed by the Tribunal, wherever they might be serving their prison terms.

Statutory determinations of the Tribunal

According to its Statute, "[t]he International Tribunal shall have the power to prosecute persons responsible for serious violations of international humanitarian law committed in the territory of the former Yugoslavia since 1991 in accordance with the provisions of the present Statute".[5]

Under the definition embraced by the Statute, a war crime is one or more of the actions constituting grave transgressions of the 12 August 1949 Geneva Conventions, including:

(a)   willful killing;
(b)   torture or inhuman treatment, including biological experiments;
(c)   willfully causing great suffering or serious injury to body or health;

(d) extensive destruction and appropriation of property, not justified by military necessity and carried out unlawfully and wantonly;
(e) compelling a prisoner of war or a civilian to serve in the forces of a hostile power;
(f) willfully depriving a prisoner of war or a civilian of the rights of fair and regular trial;
(g) unlawful deportation or transfer or unlawful confinement of a civilian;
(h) taking civilians as hostages.[6]

In addition to proscribing breaches of the Geneva Conventions, the Tribunal's Statute also criminalizes breaches of the 1907 Hague Convention on the laws and customs of war on the ground.

Such transgressions of the rules and customs of war may include:

(a) employment of poisonous weapons or other weapons calculated to cause unnecessary suffering;
(b) wanton destruction of cities, towns or villages, or devastation not justified by military necessity;
(c) attack, or bombardment, by whatever means, of undefended towns, villages, dwellings, or buildings;
(d) seizure of, destruction or willful damage done to institutions dedicated to religion, charity and education, the arts and sciences, historic monuments and works of art and science;
(e) plunder of public or private property.[7]

The Statute also specifically criminalizes genocide on the basis of the 1948 Convention on Genocide, according to which genocide is a crime regardless of where it is committed and whether in times of peace or of war. The definition of genocide is very precise:

"Genocide means any of the following acts committed with intent to destroy, in whole or in part, a national, ethnical, racial or religious group, as such:

(a) killing members of the group;
(b) causing serious bodily or mental harm to members of the group;
(c) deliberately inflicting on the group conditions of life calculated to bring about its physical destruction in whole or in part;
(d) imposing measures intended to prevent births within the group;
(e) forcibly transferring children of the group to another group."[8]

The Statute prescribes that the following actions will be subject to penalization:

(a) genocide;
(b) conspiracy to commit genocide;
(c) direct and public incitement to commit genocide;
(d) attempt to commit genocide;
(e) complicity in genocide.[9]

Similarly, the Statute envisages that the ICTY's jurisdiction will extend over the prosecution of all persons responsible for the following crimes "when committed in armed conflict, whether international or internal in character, and directed against any civilian population":

(a) murder;
(b) extermination;
(c) enslavement;
(d) deportation;
(e) imprisonment;
(f) torture;
(g) rape;
(h) persecution on political, racial and religious grounds;
(i) other inhumane acts.[10]

An important element of the regulation present in the Statute is that the ICTY will prosecute only on the basis of personal responsibility, in other words that it will not prosecute groups, collectives or organizations.

Although the above formulated principle of individual, personal responsibility seems exclusive of criminal organizations that might in some cases be considered responsible for war crimes, individual responsibility also includes the responsibility of a head of state, government official or other person in a position of authority. These consequences derive from precedents that occurred after the Second World War. They imply that a defense on the basis of immunity of a head of state, or on the basis of having engaged in the prohibited action in an official capacity, will not be a basis for release from criminal responsibility or a reduction of the penalty.

According to the Statute, a person acting in an official capacity will be held personally responsible for issuing illegal orders to commit a crime. Equally important is the provision that any such person in a position of authority will be culpable for failing to prevent a crime or preclude an illegal behavior of their subordinates. The Statute thus says:

> The fact that any of the acts referred to in articles 2 to 5 of the present Statute was committed by a subordinate does not relieve his superior of criminal responsibility if he knew or had reason to know that the subordinate was about to commit such acts or had done so and the superior failed to take the necessary and reasonable measures to prevent such acts or to punish the perpetrators thereof.[11]

This above provision enables the ICTY to prosecute the leaders who incite genocidal wars, even if they are not directly physically present in the place where crimes take place, on the basis of being or having to be aware that crimes are or were taking place, and yet tolerating them and their perpetrators. There is therefore no legal impediment to the prosecution of the leaders who have been responsible for the killings in the former Yugoslavia, whichever quarters they come from.

Many of the suspicions local political commentators in the Balkans feel towards the justice-fulfilling and reconciliation-building potential of the ICTY derives from concerns over whether the leaders responsible for massive deaths, including those from the NATO countries, will be brought to answer for their crimes, or the work of the ICTY will be restricted to lower levels of the army, political and paramilitary hierarchy. *The definitions of individual responsibility and their characterizations in the Tribunal's Statute make it legally possible, even required, for the Tribunal to prosecute the top political and military leaders who may be responsible for starting the war and who might have known of, encouraged, or ordered the atrocities.*

The statutory regulation of jurisdiction of the ICTY respects the principle *ne bis in idem*, namely that one person cannot be tried twice under the same charges. This means that persons tried for war crimes by national courts will not be tried again by the ICTY, except where the charges brought up by the national court *did not* correspond to the charges brought up by the ICTY, *or* the national courts in the relevant case did not satisfy the conditions of impartiality, independence or realistic possibility of reaching a verdict.[12]

Since, according to the Statute, the intention of the UN Security Council in establishing the ICTY was not to discourage trials by national courts, there is a probability that a conflict of jurisdiction between the national courts and the ICTY will occur. The Statute envisages that all such conflicts will be treated according to the principle that the ICTY will have superior rights and jurisdiction to those of the national courts. National courts and governments are expected to *turn over* their accused to the ICTY *at any stage in the investigation or trial process if the ICTY demands extradition.*[13]

However, in determining penalties, the ICTY will take into account the level of severity of the penalty that would be passed by a national court for the relevant crime. The ICTY is not empowered by its Statute to pass a death sentence.[14]

In addition to these provisions, there is a separate set of rules and procedures regulating the conduct of investigation and trial, the right of appeal, etc.

From all of the above considerations, it could generally be concluded that the ICTY's Statute provides a *good basis* for the fulfillment of its mission, which includes emphasizing the principle of individual responsibility for war-time atrocities and facilitating the process of reconciliation and confidence-building between the southern Balkan nations. Whether the ICTY will in fact succeed in accomplishing these tasks will to a large extent depend on its ability to affirm and preserve its impartiality, clarity of purpose and integrity. The integrity of any court is guaranteed first and foremost by the integrity of its judges and its operational, legal and financial independence of any government or interest group.

Notes

1   All these objections have been widely publicized by the Yugoslav government officials in the media since 1993.
2   See the analysis of the organization of the UN in Oudraat, C.J., "The United Nations and Internal Conflict", in Brown, M.E. (ed.), *The international dimensions of internal conflict*, MIT Press, Cambridge, Mass., 1996, pp. 489–535.
3   "Statute of the International Tribunal for the Prosecution of Persons Responsible for Serious Violations of International Humanitarian Law Committed in the Territory of the Former Yugoslavia since 1991", in *Basic Documents*, The United Nations — International Criminal Tribunal for the Former Yugoslavia, The Hague, 1995. pp. 1–28.
4   All this holds for the first phase of the Yugoslav civil wars, 1991–5.
5   Article 1, Ibid., p. 5.
6   Article 2, Ibid., pp. 5–7.

7	Article 3, Ibid., p. 7.
8	Article 4, Loc. cit.
9	Article 4, Ibid., pp. 7–9.
10	Article 5, Ibid., p. 9.
11	Article 7, Ibid., pp. 9–11.
12	"1. No person shall be tried before a national court for acts constituting serious violations of international humanitarian law under the present Statute, for which he or she has already been tried by the International Tribunal. 2. A person who has been tried by a national court for acts constituting serious violations of international humanitarian law may be subsequently tried by the international Tribunal only if: (a) the act for which he or she was tried was characterized as an ordinary crime or (b) the national court proceedings were not impartial or independent, were designed to shield the accused from international criminal responsibility, or the case was not diligently prosecuted. 3. In considering the penalty to be imposed on a person convicted of a crime under the present Statute, the International Tribunal shall take into account the extent to which any penalty imposed by a national court on the same person for the same act has already been served." — Article 10, Ibid., pp. 11–13.
13	"1. The International Tribunal and national courts shall have concurrent jurisdiction to prosecute persons for serious violations of international humanitarian law committed in the territory of the former Yugoslavia since 1 January 1991. 2. The International Tribunal shall have primacy over national courts. At any stage of the procedure the International Tribunal may formally request national courts to defer to the competence of the International Tribunal in accordance with the present Statute and the Rules of Procedure and Evidence of the International Tribunal." — Article 9, Ibid., p. 11.
14	"1. The penalty imposed by the Trial Chamber shall be limited to imprisonment. In determining the terms of imprisonment the Trial Chambers shall have recourse to the general practice regarding prison sentences in the courts of the former Yugoslavia. 2. In imposing the sentences the Trial Chambers should take into account such factors as the gravity of the offence and the individual circumstances of the convicted person. 3. In addition to imprisonment, the Trial Chambers may order the return of any property and proceeds acquired by criminal conduct, including by means of duress, to their rightful owners." — Article 24, Ibid., p. 23.

5 The First Indictments and What They Show

There are two types of indictments raised by the ICTY: public, and secret (sealed) ones. The secret indictments are the result of the ICTY's policy arising from the insight that the most controversial indictees are extremely unlikely to be captured, as long as they somehow figure in a feasibility equation of the main powers involved in the former Yugoslav area. The ICTY's officials concluded that the capture of those accused who occupied powerful positions in society would be more likely if they had not known that they were on the ICTY's "Wanted list".

This policy is deeply wrong. It is wrong on at least two counts. First, it obscures the picture of justice and threatens the confidence in a court when that court operates on a secret basis. Secrecy in judicial work (especially concerning the indictments) is contrary to the democratic and transparent spirit of justice, and as such it is bound to instill fear and suspicion towards the ICTY. Secondly, the ICTY's officials neither tried to hide the existence of a "secret list" of the accused, nor would it have been possible to hide that policy. The latest possible point in time when it would have become obvious would have been the arrest of the first persons on the secret list. The result of the policy, however, has been deeply discouraging: all those in positions of decision-making, on whatever level, in the controversial regions of the former Yugoslavia are or will soon be avoiding any contact with any representatives of international organizations, as well as any travel abroad, because of the threat of being arrested under a secret file of charges.

Most people in the former Yugoslavia believe that charges before the ICTY are not based primarily on an actual responsibility for war crimes, but either on purely political goals of the western powers, or on a summarily conceived collective responsibility of all those who belonged to the army, governance structures or even the ethnic population mainly blamed for atrocities in a certain region. So, secret indictments serve to threaten an exceeding number of people away from the ICTY and the international community, many of whom could both help the Tribunal in locating the real villains, and help their communities re-build the institutional and governance infrastructure owing to their bureaucratic, management or political experience in the former governance structures. In other words, the secret indictments achieve a counter-effect to that which they were designed for.

As they remain "secret" (although the existence of at least one, Željko Ražnatović — Arkan, with its content remaining hidden) was revealed publicly at the very beginning of April 1999, there is little that can be said about them at this stage. What can be discussed, indeed, are the first charges leveled by the tribunal, the first sentences handed down, and the manner of operation of the ICTY and its affiliated institutions.

Charges and arrests

The first person charged by the Tribunal was Dragan Nikolić, a Serb, who was charged on 4/11/1994 with grave breaches of the 1949 Geneva Conventions, violations of the laws or customs of war, and crimes against humanity. Nikolić was the only person charged by the Tribunal in 1994. He has not yet been detained or tried under these charges.

There were 15 indictments in 1995, with 43 indictees. On 13/2/1995 the following persons, all Serbs, were charged for crimes committed in the Omarska concentration camp:

(1) Željko Meakić, who was charged with grave breaches of the 1949 Geneva Conventions, violations of the laws or customs of war, genocide, and crimes against humanity;

(2) Miroslav Kvočka, charged with grave breaches of the 1949 Geneva Convention, violations of the laws or customs of war, and crimes against humanity;

(3) Dragoljub Prčac, charged with the same crimes as above;

(4) Mladen Radić, same as above;

(5) Milojica Kos, same as above;

(6) Momčilo Gruban, same as above;

(7) Dušan Knežević, same as above, plus Knežević was also charged on 21/7/1995 in the indictment known as "Sikirica & others" for the same crimes committed in the Keraterm concentration camp;

(8) Zoran Žigić, same as above, also charged along with Knežević for the same crimes in the Keraterm camp.

Of those accused, Meakić, Kvočka, Prčac, Radić, Kos and Gruban were also charged with command responsibility for crimes committed by their subordinates which they knew or were due to know of, and yet failed to prevent them and punish their perpetrators.

As of 24/7/1998, when this list was last updated, half of them had been detained: Kvočka and Radić were detained by international forces in Bosnia on 8/4/1998, Milojica Kos was detained by international forces on 28/5/1998, and Zoran Žigić surrendered voluntarily on 16/4/1998. In May 1998, Chief Prosecutor Louise Arbour withdrew charges against Momčilo Gruban, meaning that he is now a free man, while the remaining three — Meakić, Prčac and Knežević — were at large.[1]

The second indictment in 1995 was that of "Tadić & others", which was initially raised on 13/2/1995, and on 14/12/1995. It involves charges against Duško Tadić and Goran Borovnica for grave breaches of the 1949 Geneva Conventions, violations of the laws and customs of war, and crimes against humanity. Tadić was arrested on 13/2/1994 in Munich, Germany. A guilty verdict was reached on 7/5/1997, and he was convicted to 20 years imprisonment on 14/7/1997. The appeals procedure was ongoing as of 24/7/1998. Borovnica had not been arrested and was at large.

The third 1995 indictment was that of "Sikirica and others", brought forward on 21/7/1995 for crimes committed in the Keraterm camp. The indictees were the following:

(1) Duško Sikirica, indicted for grave breaches of the 1949 Geneva Conventions, violations of wars and customs of war, genocide, and crimes against humanity. Sikirica was also charged with command responsibility for war crimes;

(2) Damir Dosen, charged with grave breaches of the 1949 Geneva Conventions, violations of the laws or customs of war, crimes against humanity, and command responsibility for war crimes;

(3) Dragan Fustar, accused of the same crimes as above;

(4) Dragan Kulundžija, indicted for the same as above;

(5) Nenad Banović, accused of grave breaches of the 1949 Geneva Conventions, violations of the laws and customs of war, and crimes against humanity;

(6) Predrag Banović, same as above;

(7) Dušan Knežević, same as above (also accused of the same crimes in the Omarska Camp on 13/2/1995 — "Meakić & others") and

(8) Zoran Žigić, same as above. Of those accused in the "Sikirica & others" indictment, only Simo Zarić surrendered on 24/2/1998, and is now detained.

The fourth indictment in 1995 was that of "Miljković & others", raised on 21/7/1995 for crimes committed in Bosanski Šamac. The indictment included:

(1) Slobodan Miljković, accused of grave breaches of the 1949 Geneva Conventions, violations of the laws or customs of war, and crimes against humanity;
(2) Blagoje Simić, same as above, plus command responsibility for war crimes;
(3) Milan Simić, indicted for grave breaches of the 1949 Geneva Conventions, violations of the laws or customs of war, and crimes against humanity;
(4) Miroslav Tadić, charged for grave breaches of the 1949 Geneva Conventions and crimes against humanity;
(5) Stevan Todorović, charged for grave breaches of the 1949 Geneva Conventions, violations of the laws or customs of war, and crimes against humanity, and
(6) Simo Zarić, indicted for grave breaches of the 1949 Geneva Conventions and crimes against humanity.

Of those indicted in the "Miljković & others" case, Milan Simić and Miroslav Radić surrendered on 14/2/1998, and Simo Zarić surrendered on 24/2/1998. Milan Simić was provisionally released on 26 March 1998, due to return to The Hague and surrender himself into the custody of the Tribunal two weeks before the beginning of the trial (on 24/7/1998 no date was set yet). The others were still at large.

The fifth 1995 indictment was the one of "Jelisić & other", on 21/7/1995, for crimes committed in and around Brčko. Goran Jelisić was charged for grave breaches of the 1949 Geneva Conventions, violations of the laws or customs of war, genocide, and crimes against humanity, while Ranko Cesić was accused of grave breaches of the 1949 Geneva Conventions, violations of the laws and customs of war, and crimes against humanity. Goran Jelisić was detained by international forces on 22/1/1998. Ranko Cesić remained at large.

The sixth 1995 indictment was that of Milan Martić, brought forward on 25/7/1995 for violations of the laws or customs of war. Martić, who was the Minister of the Interior of Republika Srpska Krajina in Croatia, had not been taken into custody.

The seventh 1995 indictment was that of Radovan Karadžić and Ratko Mladić, both accused of grave breaches of the 1949 Geneva Conventions, violations of the laws or customs of war, genocide, and crimes against humanity, along with command responsibility for war crimes. Both were also separately indicted on 16/11/1995 under the "Srebrenica" indictment. Both Karadžić and Mladić were at large.

The seventh indictment in 1995 was that of Ivica Rajić, who was charged for grave breaches of the 1949 Geneva Conventions and violations of the laws and customs of war — crimes allegedly committed in Stupni Do. On 24/7/1998, Rajić was at large.

The eight 1995 indictment was the indictment of "Mrkšić & others" for crimes committed in and around Vukovar Hospital. The indictment was raised on 7/11/1995, and subsequently amended on 3/4/1996 and on 2/12/1997. Mile Mrkšić, Miroslav Radić and Veselin Šljivančanin were charged for grave breaches of the 1949 Geneva Conventions, violations of the laws and customs of war, and crimes against humanity. All remain at large.

The next indictment was that of Tihomir Blaškić, initially raised on 10/11/1995, and subsequently amended on 28/11/1996 and 25/4/1997, for crimes committed in the Lašva Valley, in Bosnia. Blaškić was indicted for grave breaches of the 1949 Geneva Conventions, violations of the laws or customs of war, crimes against humanity, and command responsibility for war crimes. Blaškić voluntarily surrendered to the Tribunal on 1/4/1996.

The following was the indictment of "Kordić & others" for crimes in the Lašva Valley, raised on 10/11/1995. It included cases against:

(1) Dario Kordić, accused of grave breaches of the 1949 Geneva Conventions, violations of the laws or customs of war, crimes against humanity, and command responsibility for war crimes;
(2) Mario Čerkez, accused of grave breaches of the 1949 Geneva Conventions, violations of the laws or customs of war, and command responsibility for war crimes, and
(3) Zlatko Aleksovski, who stands accused of the same crimes as above.

Kordić and Čerkez surrendered to the Tribunal on 6/10/1997, while Aleksovski was arrested on 8/6/1996 in Split, Croatia.

The next was the indictment of Zoran Marinić, who was accused of grave breaches of the 1949 Geneva Conventions and violations of the laws or customs of war. The indictment was raised on 10/11/1995 and as of 24/7/1998 Marinić was at large.

On 10/11/1995, the Chief Prosecutor brought forward an indictment of "Kupreškić & others", for crimes committed in the Lašva Valley. In it, Zoran Kupreškić, Mirjan Kupreškić, Vlatko Kupreškić, Vladimir Šantić, Drago Josipović, and Dragan Papić were accused of grave breaches of the 1949 Geneva Conventions and violations of the laws or customs of war.

Zoran and Mirjan Kupreškić, Šantić, Josipović and Papić surrendered to the Tribunal on 6/10/1997, while Vlatko Kupreškić was detained by international forces on 18/12/1997. The "Kupreškić & others" indictment was confirmed on 10/11/1995, but it was kept confidential until its unsealing on 27/6/1996.

On the same date as the raising of the previous indictment, Anto Furundžija was also indicted for crimes committed in the Lašva Valley, namely for grave breaches of the 1949 Geneva Conventions and for violations of the laws or customs of war. The indictment was kept sealed until 18/12/1997.

The final indictment in 1995 was the "Srebrenica" indictment, raised on 16/11/1995, against Radovan Karadžić and Ratko Mladić for violations of the laws or customs of war, genocide, crimes against humanity, and command responsibility for war crimes. As already said, both remained at large.

1996 saw three indictments, namely "Delalić and others", raised on 21/3/1996 for crimes committed in Čelebići, "Erdemović", raised on 29/5/1996, and "Gagović and others", raised on 26/6/1096 for crimes committed in and around Foča. There were 13 indictees under the 1996 indictments.

The first indictment included cases against:

(1) Zejnil Delalić, accused of grave breaches of the 1949 Geneva Conventions, violations of the laws or customs of war, and command responsibility for war crimes;
(2) Zdravko Mucić, accused of the same as above;
(3) Hazim Delić, accused of the same as above, and
(4) Esad Landzo, accused of grave breaches of the 1949 Geneva Conventions and violations of the laws or customs of war.

All the four accused were arrested — Mucić and Delalić on 18/3/1996, and Delić and Landzo on 2/5/1996. Mucić was arrested in Vienna, Delalić in Munich, Delić and Landzo in Bosnia and Herzegovina.

In the second indictment, Dražen Erdemović was charged on 29/5/1996 for violations of the laws or customs of war, and crimes against humanity. Erdemović was arrested on 2/3/1996 in the Federal Republic of Yugoslavia. He pleaded guilty to war crimes and was sentenced to 5 years imprisonment on 5/3/1998.

The third and final indictment in 1996 included the following cases:

(1) Dragan Gagović, accused of grave breaches of the 1949 Geneva Conventions, violations of the laws or customs of war, crimes against humanity, and command responsibility for war crimes;
(2) Gojko Janković, accused of the same as above;
(3) Janko Janjić, indicted for grave breaches of the 1949 Geneva Conventions, violations of the laws or customs of war, and crimes against humanity;
(4) Radomir Kovač, indicted for the same as above;
(5) Zoran Vuković, accused of the same as above;
(6) Dragan Zelenović, same as above;
(7) Dragoljub Kunarac, accused of grave violations of the 1949 Geneva Conventions, violations of the laws or customs of war, crimes against humanity, and command responsibility for war crimes, and
(8) Radovan Stanković, indicted for grave breaches of the 1949 Geneva Conventions, violations of the laws or customs of war, and crimes against humanity.

Of the eight accused, only Dragoljub Kunarac surrendered to the Tribunal on 4/3/1998. The rest remained at large.

There were only two indictments *raised by* the Tribunal in 1997.[2] They were the "Kovačević" and "Krnjojelac" indictments, brought forward on 13/3/1997 (with a subsequent redaction of the indictment on 12/5/1998 and an amendment on 23/6/1998) and on 17/6/1997, respectively. The first involved the accusation of Milan Kovačević for genocide and command responsibility for war crimes. In the second indictment, Milorad Krnjojelac was indicted for grave breaches of the 1949 Geneva Conventions, violations of the laws or customs of war, crimes against humanity, and command responsibility for war crimes. Both cases were brought up under "secret" charges. The first indictment was kept sealed until 10/7/1997, and the second was unsealed on 15/6/1998. Milan Kovačević was detained by international forces on 10/7/1997, and Milorad Krnjojelac was detained on 15/6/1998.

There were several controversies in the Tribunal's work. The first one to be discussed here, and possibly the most important one, was the death of Slavko Dokmanović. The second one concerns controversies over the withdrawal of charges against Goran Lajić and his release.

The suicide of Slavko Dokmanović

Mr. Slavko Dokmanović, a former Mayor of Vukovar, was a controversial detainee. He was arrested in Vukovar in a highly controversial manner by being invited to a meeting with General Jacques Klein, the UN Transitional Representative for managing "the peaceful transition" of Serb-controlled Republika Srpska Krajina" under Croatian control. After Mr. Dokmanović had arrived to the meeting, he entered Klein's car. The car was subsequently locked and Dokmanović was arrested and transported to The Hague. His indictment had been a secret, sealed one.

The trial of Slavko Dokmanović was also highly controversial. The evidence against him was based on assertions that he had been present at the scene of one of the war crimes in Vukovar, but in the concluding phase of the trial photographic evidence surfaced, placing Dokmanović elsewhere in Vukovar when the war crime in questions occurred.

Dokmanović committed suicide by hanging himself in his cell on the night of 28 to 29 June 1998. The suicide took place three days after the completion of the trial, and seven days before the announcement of the verdict. As a consequence, an internal inquiry "on the circumstances surrounding the death of the detainee" was ordered by the Tribunal's President, Gabrielle Kirk McDonald. The enquiry was assigned to Judge Almiro Rodrigues, who took just a few weeks to complete it, and presented his final report on 21 July 1998. There are serious problems and inconsistencies in this report.

The purposes of the report were to elucidate two points:

(1) whether any individual responsibility, including criminal negligence, was involved in Dokmanović's death "in light of the existing Rules of Detention concerning the security and safety of the detainees", and
(2) to determine whether these rules should be amended so as to avoid future repetitions of prison suicides like Dokmanović's.

The official findings of Judge Ramires' enquiry are the following:

"1. Mr. Dokmanović was suffering from depression and, for that reason, was under particular medical care;
2. From about 23 June 1998, Mr. Dokmanović was checked every half-hour, during low service hours;
3. Under the rules of the Detention Unit, a detainee may keep in his possession all clothes and personal items for his own use or consumption unless, in the opinion of the Commanding Officer or the General Director, such items constitute a threat to the security or good order of the detention unit or the host prison, or to the health or safety of any person therein;
4. This is the reason why items such as cutlery, ties, shoe laces, electric and manual razors, electric cables, are among those commonly found in a detainee's cell and were found in Mr. Dokmanović's as well;
5. On the night from 28 to 29 June 1998, after 10.00 p.m., Mr. Dokmanović twice attempted to commit suicide *by trying to cut his veins with a razor blade and by attempting to hang himself using a tie*;
6. These attempts were not visible to the guards checking the cell. This check consists of opening the little window on the cell door and looking through it into the cell. If the guard notices something unusual or abnormal, he must call at least one other guard to be present before opening the cell door itself. *On the date in question, nothing unusual was detected until midnight*;
7. *Between 11.30 P.M. and 00.05 a.m., Mr. Dokmanović short-circuited the general power supply of his cell by placing the two extreme prongs of a fork (the middle prongs of which had been deliberately bent) into one of the wall sockets. He did that in order to avoid the regular half-hour guards checking his cell*;
8. Finally, he managed to hang himself by fastening on to the top door hinge of his cell's wardrobe the end of a second tie that he had firmly attached around his neck; Mr. Dokmanović was found dead shortly after midnight;
9. All of the Rules of the Detention Unit concerning Security were observed. No negligent behavior was identified;
10. The investigation conducted did not evidence any sign of violence either at the scene of the incident or on the body of Mr. Dokmanović that would suggest a criminal act."[3]

The objections to this report, and the behavior of the Tribunal, are the following:

(1) The supervision described is not the most intense supervision available. After the last consultation with his client, Mr. Dokmanović's attorney was alarmed by Mr. Dokmanović's state of mind, as reportedly Mr. Dokmanović had suggested that he might commit suicide. Namely, during a meeting on the occasion of the attorney's last visit, he had reportedly written on a piece of paper "I am a dead man", and proceeded to cross it off. Mr. Fila's staff lodged an official warning with the Tribunal's Detention Unit, requesting maximum supervision. The closest supervision involves a 24-hour watch by means of a closed circuit TV. Despite the warning, this measure was not applied.

(2) Point 5 of the Report mentions that Mr. Dokmanović had first tried to kill himself by cutting his veins with a razor blade and by attempting to hang himself with a tie. These attempts reportedly took place between 10.00 p.m. and midnight on 28 June, yet in Point 6 of the Report it is said that "nothing unusual" was detected until midnight. Mr. Dokmanović was trying to commit suicide in a cell, in at least two ways, including cutting his veins, which would have produced large quantities of blood over his body, and by hanging himself, which would have produced a certain amount of noise, in the course of over *two hours*, and the *half-hourly checks* "failed" to raise any suspicions.

(3) In Point 7, it is said that roughly between 11.30 and midnight Mr. Dokmanović had short-circuited the power supply in his cell by a fork, in order to avoid the half-hourly watch. Yet, in Point 6 it is stated that until midnight nothing unusual had been detected. In other words, the short-circuit in power supply was not detected at all until Mr. Dokmanović succeeded in killing himself.

These are major inconsistencies, and there are two possible conclusions: either the half-hour watch was not properly observed by the guards of the Detention Unit, or the guards deliberately failed to prevent Mr. Dokmanović from killing himself. As one lawyer who participated in Mr. Dokmanović's defense said, "they simply let him kill himself". The Report, indeed, makes that clear. The conclusion in Point 9 of the Report that there was no negligence involved is most directly incriminating for the whole Tribunal.

The proceedings against Slavko Dokmanović were terminated on 15 July 1998, without the verdict ever being pronounced.

Wrongful arrests

On 5/5/1998 and 8/5/1998, the Prosecutor withdrew charges against Zdravko Govedarica, Momčilo Gruban, Predrag Kostić, Nedeljko Paspalj, Milan Pavlić, Milutin Popović, Draženko Predojević, Željko Savić, Mirko Babić, Nikica Janjić, and Dragomir Šaponja in the "Omarska" indictment, as well as against Nikica Janjić, Dragan Kandić, Goran Lajić, Dragomir Šaponja, and Nedjeljko Timarac.

These people had been wrongly indicted. Their jobs, families, social positions and life-plans suffered gravely because of the indictments, and yet they are not entitled to civil suits against the Tribunal, seeking compensation for damages, because the United Nations enjoys immunity from civil proceedings for wrongful arrest, and the ICTY was established and operates under the auspices of the United Nations.

This means that officials of the Tribunal have free hands to victimize anyone they might vaguely suspect of war crimes, thereby ruining the lives of those wrongly accused, without ever having to answer for their poorly founded accusations, even by granting financial compensation to the victims.

Goran Lajić, for example, had been detained in The Hague for 3 months before charges against him were withdrawn on the grounds that it was totally unclear "which" Goran Lajić had allegedly taken part in violations of the international humanitarian law in Keraterm, in Bosnia and Herzegovina. Lajić's defense simply produced several birth certificates from the relevant geographic area for various persons by the name of Goran Lajić, of similar age, any one of whom could have been the person accused of war crimes. The Goran Lajić who was in custody at The Hague was subsequently released.

After the release, Lajić attempted to commence legal proceedings for compensation of the damages arising from the wrongful indictment and arrest, but his attorney soon received a response from the Tribunal, quoting UN regulations absolving the Tribunal of any responsibility for civil damages arising from wrongful indictments and arrests.

The two cases, the mockingly inadequate handling of the Dokmanović suicide and the ICTY's being at liberty to arrest and release without having to answer for miscarriages of justice, illustrate potentially fatal problems in the legitimacy of the ICTY's work. These circumstances and manner of operation of the ICTY have the potential to cancel any credibility the Tribunal might have in the former Yugoslavia.

Conclusions

The ICTY has so far demonstrated little or no divergence from the foreign policies of the great powers, especially the USA. There are very compromising legal regulations governing the work of the ICTY, not least those absolving it of civil liabilities for miscarriages of justice, which was demonstrated in the case of Goran Lajić. Any court that is not liable for miscarriages of justice is granted intolerable latitude. Such a broad mandate, without the usual checks imposed by civil liabilities, constitutes a serious threat to human rights, which the ICTY was allegedly created to protect.

The institutional checks within the Tribunal are clearly also inadequate. Sufficient evidence for this is the poorly supervised treatment of prisoners in the Tribunal's Detention Unit, which made possible the death of Slavko Dokmanović. Particularly worrying in this instance is the cynical report by Judge Rodrigues, which was the result of the internal inquiry into Dokmanović's death.

The first case brought up by the Tribunal included only two political leaders, namely Radovan Karadžić and Ratko Mladić, and neither of those has been arrested. Most of those charged have been junior-to-middle ranking officers, up to the rank of unit and camp commander, namely the individuals who were in the middle or at the end of the chain of responsibility for war crimes, the chain having been described earlier. These first indictments show a lack of clear orientation of the ICTY concerning its mission, the main principles it should follow, and the importance of responsibility and accountability of judicial institutions.

Notes

1   By the time this book is out of print, many of the data contained here will change: some indictees will be apprehended, some will be convicted, some acquitted, some will, perhaps, die. However, this does not affect the purpose of this analysis. In almost 4 years of operation of the Tribunal, from its establishment until 24/7/1998, when the data this analysis is based on were last updated, enough time had passed for the main directions and policies of the Tribunal to develop and crystallize, thus sufficiently illuminating the topic of "the first indictments and what they show". This was a key period in the Tribunal's work that largely determined its performance in light of the compromises and principles mentioned in

Chapter 2, and thus also its prospects and capacity to help generate reconciliation in the former Yugoslavia.

2   The syntagm "raised by" the Tribunal instead of the usual "raised before" the Tribunal is appropriate here, because the Office of the Prosecutor is an organizational part of the ICTY. Normally, the prosecution is an independent organ from the court itself, in which case it would appropriately bring indictments *before* the Tribunal for its consideration. The ICTY is an exception to the normal practice — it brings indictments forward itself, namely this is done by an Office of the Prosecutor that is an organizational *part of the Tribunal*.

3   Report issued on 21/7/1998 in The Hague, signed by Judge Almiro Rodrigues, and published on the Internet — http://www.un.org/icty/bulletin21/dokman.htm (1/4/1999). Italics added by Aleksandar Fatić.

6 Crimes and Responsibility in a Civil War

Civil war blurs many distinctions that are otherwise clear, both in politics and in criminology. The reason for the blurring is in the interplay between law and politics. Concepts and legal characterizations that otherwise usually coincide, tend to differ in meaning in a civil war. Perhaps the key such discrepancy is between blame and responsibility.

Responsibility and guilt

Political considerations dictate that, in order for a post-settlement reconciliation process to be successful, guilt must be determined as individual, rather than collective. This doesn't mean, however, that collectives don't have a *causal responsibility* for the atrocities for which *guilt* is ascribed individually. Ethnic and other collectives often legitimize the perpetration of atrocities by supporting various criminal policies of genocide and ethnic cleansing.

A certain amount of causal responsibility for wartime atrocities is always attached to all those who have either actively participated in, supported, or could have prevented the atrocities, but did not do so. Large sections of ethnically homogenized and radicalized populations in many civil wars do have an amount of responsibility for the war time atrocities committed by their side, because, assuming that they knew of such atrocities, they could have presumably prevented them by organized action. In this context, even if entire populations who at least tolerate war crimes committed by their troops or troops acting nominally "in their name" do have a *theoretical* responsibility for those crimes, it is clear that the *practicalities* of civil war situations make it difficult to assign any tangible blame to the whole population. Yet, some experiences from the civil wars in the Balkans suggest a collective participation in war-mongering policies.

In practice, fear rules in any civil conflict, and the most violent, deviant elements in society come to the surface, both driving the horrendous violent campaigns, and oppressing all those within their own ranks who disagree with, or might protest against the violence. For those who are not in the uniform or in local power structures, it is almost impossible, and certainly highly risky for their own security and that of their families, to oppose the criminal campaigns conducted by their elected or self-proclaimed minority "elites". So, although one cannot plausibly argue that there is no such thing as collective responsibility for war time atrocities, from a practical point of view much more clearly noticeable, and much more important and useful for judicial treatment, is individual and group responsibility for war crimes. This narrower concept of responsibility coincides with guilt and blame. Those who have directly contributed to the perpetration of atrocities are also the guilty ones for those atrocities.

International war crimes tribunals typically start with the trying of immediate executors, or those that most clearly satisfy the above requirement. That is connected with one of the main moral problems associated with the work of war crimes tribunals.

War crimes typically take place within a *policy* of war. This is especially true in civil wars. To start a civil war, in most cases, at least two pre-conditions must be created: (i) differences between the groups potentially in conflict must *be escalated* to the extent that makes *armed* conflict the most likely result, and (ii) the groups themselves must *be rallied* or homogenized behind a common identity, which is often largely artificial, while the intra-group differences must be diminished to the point of being unnoticeable. The differences, so the experience in most civil wars shows, tend to be deliberately *blown out of proportion* by the national or other group elites. Similarly, masses rarely spontaneously *rally* behind those elements of common identity or interests that tend to cause civil wars. Rather they are *driven* by their elites to homogenize around confrontational positions towards other groups.

The wars in the former Yugoslavia, especially those in Bosnia and Croatia, illustrated this point quite well. The ruling communist elites used their monopoly over the media, army and police to create a disintegrating inferno where all mutual bonds between the Serbs, Croats and Muslims were forgotten, and fear and hatred took over. In fact, everybody was afraid of everybody else, most of all of what their own state and political elite might do to them. This was a phenomenon typical of the sudden disappearance of all citizens' control over the state. In such a chaos of fear, the only one common enemy and source of fear that everybody was *allowed* to identify was the other national group. Those who inflicted fear at the same time imposed the identity of the other national group as a legitimate, declarable and common, although, of course, quite false, *source of fear*. And thus the manipulation of national feelings started.

In this context, it is quite easy to see how national elites actually *manufactured* the civil war(s) in the former Yugoslavia as a means for releasing the energy that should have, in normal transitional circumstances, destroyed or deposed *them*. In those transitional countries that did not plunge into civil war the same energy was used to effect changes of the political system.

The wars were designed to be criminal — they were civilian onto a civilian, paramilitary criminal unit onto a village, army onto a city, terrorist group onto conscripted and disarmed young soldiers in disarray and without effective command. The stage for the killing fields was set in advance. Every crime that took place within that criminal campaign must be viewed not only as the fault of the immediate executors, *but at least as much* as the fault of the national elites. Before the full-scale beginning of the Yugoslav wars, Croatian Minister for the Interior, General Martin Špegelj was captured on film red handed with a fully developed plan for the Croatian Ministry of the Interior to slaughter army officers and their families living in Croatia.

The concept of collective responsibility of nations for what those who act "on their behalf" do in a war has not always been ruled out in the "international community's" handling of the Yugoslav crisis. The concept of collective blame is inherent in imposing international sanctions on entire nations. One of the clearest expressions of this was the Statement to the International Conference on the former Yugoslavia in Geneva, on 16 December, 1992, by the then US Secretary of State, Laurence Eagleburger, which reads:

> We have, on the one hand, a moral and historical obligation not to stand back a second time in this century. while a people faces obliteration. But we have also, I believe, a political obligation to the people of Serbia to signal clearly the risk they currently run of sharing the inevitable fate of those who practice ethnic cleansing in their name.

Clearly, those who commit a crime of war are guilty and must be tried, but at the same time, perhaps less clearly, those behind the political levers of power in a civil war are equally guilty or guiltier. Eagleburger has also depicted this notion in the above quoted speech, in the following words:

The fact of the matter is that we know that crimes against humanity have occurred, and we know when and where they occurred. We know, moreover, which forces committed those crimes, and under whose command they operated. *And we know, finally, who the political leaders are to whom those military commanders were — and still are — responsible.*[1]

Even if the population had voted for an explicit policy that eventually led to war, the democratic shield of legitimization must not be a wall impenetrable by criminal responsibility. Whether supported by the population or not, those who tolerate, encourage or cause war crimes should be held as criminally responsible as the immediate executors should, or more so. While there might be an element of collective responsibility in the collective "democratic" legitimization of warmongering national elites, the practicalities of ascribing criminal guilt to collectives are so complex and depend on so many elements, that it would be counterproductive to assign collective culpability to entire nations. At the same time, had it not been for the leaders, the atrocities, in most cases, would not have happened, and it is quite simple and productive for peace to assign individual culpability to political and military leaders.

Those directly involved in the perpetration of a war crime, their accomplices or those who could have prevented the war crime but did not do so, are the ones who are typically accused the first. But those who had made the crime probable in the first place (e.g. those who had demonized the other group in the media, those who called for war, and their political masters) are at least as guilty and need to be accused as soon as possible after the immediate perpetrators are.

Criminal responsibility bears upon those immediately associated with the crime, both before and after the occurrence of the crime (those involved in its preparation or those who had known of its preparation or intent to commit it, but had failed to take reasonable action to prevent it) and those who, afterwards, failed to identify the crime and the perpetrators and to punish them, although they were able to do so. *In addition*, criminal responsibility for each war crime *goes back* in time, *through* any shield of "democratic" political legitimization, and equally bears upon the key political leaders who were responsible for the war and their immediate political and military surroundings. Only if an international war crimes tribunal is able to assert such consistent justice and identify the ones who are guilty for the bloodshed but who would otherwise escape justice, does it make sense and will it be accepted as an impartial international actor by the local populations. Only if international tribunals are so accepted can they help effect reconciliation in the lands torn by civil war.

The moral problem in the accepted practice of the war crimes tribunals' work is that the lines of responsibility that coincides with guilt rarely ever penetrate the democratic (smoke) screen of legitimization of policies that lead to atrocious wars, and when they do, they get to the key political leaders only after all the others, who are less guilty, are tried and penalized. In the meantime, the key villains usually provoke new sufferings and atrocities, often start new wars, and grow old surrounded by the "good life".

Political power *structurally shields* those whose moral guilt for war time atrocities is the greatest, while exposing to prosecution those who, although guilty, are less so than the key political leader. Thus, while responsibility in a civil war appears unavoidably to some extent divergent with actual criminal guilt, the main problem is that, paradoxically, the widest realm of causal responsibility (the "responsible" part of the population), which the practical judicial action never reaches, at the same time appears to protect those whose responsibility should ideally be addressed *first* in the form of criminal guilt. This is where the room for abuse of political power in quasi-democracies affected by civil war lies. That is the most difficult political problem facing international war crimes courts.

To penetrate through the screen of democratic legitimization and arrest the key political leaders who are primarily guilty for the war and war-time atrocities is seen as opening a "can of worms" and international organizations and foreign intervenors usually shy away from doing this. Such action requires a heavy commitment of troops, political will in distant countries for a lasting coercive presence in the crisis area, and a sustained and consistent global approach to pursue all those who incite wars. Because of constellations of political favoritism, many powerful countries avoid committing themselves to such consistency and judicial decision.

A war crime

To be able to discuss the realms of guilt and responsibility for any particular type and instance of war atrocity, one must first have a clear concept of what a war atrocity, or a war crime, is.

War in itself is a big atrocity, resulting in massive killing, destruction and displacement, among other evils. But within a war, a war crime is an action committed contrary to the habits of war, particularly appalling in its brutality. The most widespread war crimes are the killing and torture of civilians and prisoners of war, destruction of civilian settlements, "ethnic cleansing" and displacement of civilian populations, mistreatment of refugees, etc.

Because of the context in which war crimes occur, their detection depends on witnesses who speak out, sometimes they include low-ranking perpetrators who decide to confess years after the crimes had taken place. Such confessions are always difficult to manage, because various, often psychopathic, immediate executors are under hierarchic command or "hierarchic tolerance" by regular officers, whom they incriminate by their testimonies. These officers are under hierarchic command or tolerance by politicians, and once they are arrested, they will incriminate the politicians. In this way, the spiral of criminal responsibility for a war crime unfolds. This is what international war crimes tribunals hope for, but it is also what makes their mission difficult.

War crimes, in the context of leading to incrimination, are somewhat different from ordinary crimes. As they occur in a war, they are usually committed within an explicit hierarchic responsibility which, when traced back by an international war crimes court, reaches the highest levels of the military and political establishment. This hierarchic aspect of criminal responsibility for war crimes has a direct consequence for the description of a war crime: as war criminals are not only the immediate executors, but also those who order or tolerate actions that result in war crimes, a war crime is not, by inference, only an action of killing, torching, raping, etc., but also an order to that effect, or a political action either expressly aimed at producing such a consequence, or of which such a consequence was a foreseeable likely result. In other words, there is an important difference between an ordinary crime and a war crime in that, in an ordinary crime, inducing someone to directly commit a crime is a lesser crime than the actual crime committed under inducement (because the one induced to commit a crime, presumably, does not have to commit it, although he or she might be persuaded to do so). On the other hand, inducement to commit a war crime can be seen as a war crime of equal or greater gravity than the actual commission of the action (because, within a military, paramilitary, or informal hierarchy in a war, one cannot really *not* commit the crime in the same sense as one can refuse to commit an ordinary crime). If the actual executor is a soldier acting under orders, or a paramilitary trooper, then refusal entails considerable risk to oneself. If, on the other hand, the executor is a "volunteer", a psychopath acting on self-initiative, then those who allow such a crime to happen within a military campaign, let alone if they directly tolerate it, are equally responsible.

A war crime is therefore a much more flexible and wide concept than an ordinary crime. It has an important political dimension. The commanding officer in any controversial military action has a responsibility to protect the helpless prisoners and civilians. Even if he does not shoot them himself, or if he does not expressly order their killing, he is guilty of their murder because, had he not tolerated it, it would not have occurred. The same applies to politicians who act as "commanders in chief" of international military and paramilitary forces that commit wartime atrocities.

Unfolding the spiral — getting a hold of the villain

At the beginning of November 1997, a fifty-year old Serbian volunteer in the Croatian and Bosnian wars by the name of Slobodan Mišić, nicknamed "Top" ("Cannon", in translation), shocked the Serbian public by giving a statement to a local paper about having killed "between seventy and eighty" people in the civil war in Bosnia.[2] None of the killings were in a battle, most of those reportedly murdered were civilians, including women, and all the killings described were apparently committed in a war-crime manner. Mišić gave exact locations, dates and names of the commanding officers. Although cautioned by the interviewing journalist, after he had given the statement, that he could be arrested if the statement was published, he instructed the paper to go ahead and publish the statement, because he "would not let himself be captured alive". The next day he was arrested.

Mišić's case is typical, for there must be thousands of people like him, who feel severely marginalized after the war, and who will decide to attract attention to themselves by breaking the silence, even at the cost of being sent to prison.[3]

Having grown up in an orphanage, Mišić spent a life of marginalization: released from the obligatory army-service due to "incapacity for service", he became a boxer for a local club, and was a long-time unemployed. After having seen the war-mongering reports of Croatian crimes against Serbs on Belgrade Television, he allegedly joined a volunteer unit under the active command of the Yugoslav Army, and committed horrendous crimes in organized campaigns against civilians, particularly against Muslim villages in Bosnia, where he went after

Croatia. "I only hope that trouble erupts in Kosovo", he said at the end of the interview. "I don't feel regrets for what I have done — I only feel sorry that I killed two Muslim women between the ages of twenty-five and twenty-six. They were dressed in jogging suits, I didn't even see they were women. The next morning I saw that they were women who had been looking for some food."[4]

Mišić's story has since been disputed, but it is exemplary in many ways. Apart from clearly exhibiting psychopathic traits, Mišić may well be a symbol of who war criminals often are. Civil war brings to the surface the worst members of society, and those who give them arms and send them to do what Mišić allegedly did commit, according to the earlier analysis, war crimes of their own, that are graver than the crimes of those who actually pulled the triggers.

Mišić and similar alleged low-rank murderers would surely help start the spiral of responsibility if they are brought to answer for their actions before an international tribunal. They want attention and exposure because, being marginalized and disappointed as many "war veterans" tend to be, they feel that they have little to lose.

There should be no confusion about one thing, however. Most reports about war crimes committed in the former Yugoslavia cite reported Serbian crimes. There was a general impression in the West during the Yugoslav wars that Serbian forces committed most war crimes. This may or may not be so. It cannot be emphasized enough that the proportion between the numbers of war crimes committed by each of the three national groups can only be established after *all* perpetrators are indiscriminately tried and convicted. By the time the process arrives to that stage, the national reconciliation may well be underway so far that few would really still care about which particular national group most of the war criminals came from.

All sides in the Yugoslav wars were probably involved in the perpetration of war atrocities. Croatian General Tihomir Blaškić is currently being tried for genocide of Muslim civilians in the Lašva Valley. Court files from the Sarajevo criminal courts show horrific crimes committed against the innocent Serbian residents of Sarajevo who had stayed in the city during the siege of it. At that time Bosnian criminals such as Juka Prazina and a certain Musan Topalović — Caco were placed in charge of the city's defense. Their paramilitary units, formerly criminal gangs with thick police records, had a free reign over the helpless Serbian residents of Sarajevo. Musan Topalović — Caco is known to have savagely murdered kidnapped Serbian civilians. He and his troops were responsible for torture, rape, beheading, throat slitting, and a range of horrendous crimes over Sarajevo's Serbs during the siege. Musan Topalović was eventually hunted down and killed by the Bosnian police, because he had started to represent a threat even to his own. The Bosnian judicial authorities now hold reports and sworn statements by witnesses of his crimes and those of his gang. This illustrates that the pursuit of those accused of war crimes should not in any way be connected with seeking to identify which national group has committed most war time atrocities. The former is a moral and judicial task. The latter is a political assessment. By the time the former task is fulfilled, it is questionable how relevant, sought after, or productive the latter would be.

Notes

1 Italic added by the author.
2 See "I killed between 70 and 90 people", *Danas*, 6 November 1997, reprinted from the local paper *Vranjske novine*.
3 Paradoxically, if tried for genocide under the Yugoslav criminal jurisdiction, Mišić and other killers can only be sentenced to a limited prison sentence, because war crimes are sanctioned under the Federal Yugoslav criminal law, which allows neither the death penalty, nor life-imprisonment. At the same time, other crimes, notably "aggravated murder" and "aggravated robbery with a deadly consequence", carry the possibility of passing a death sentence, because they are not federal crimes, but ones sanctioned under the criminal legislation of one of the two constituent republics, Serbia and Montenegro. The criminal laws of Serbia and Montenegro, unlike the federal criminal law, are not as yet equalized with the Yugoslav Constitution, and they allow the death penalty. Thus the paradox that, conditionally speaking, "less grave" crimes are sanctioned more severely than the gravest crime of genocide. The Yugoslav government has been attempting to resolve this contradiction by creating a new federal criminal law, which has been long announced and which is to override the republican laws.
4 When this chapter was first being written, it was noted here that "Kosovo is Serbia's southernmost province, populated by 90% ethnic Albanians, strongly independence-minded. According to most analysts of the Balkans, Kosovo is the next and most dangerous flash point of civil conflict in Europe (See Fatić, A., "Kosovo and eastern European democratization: Solving an indigestible problem", lecture to the Danube-River of Cooperation conference, held in October 1997 at the Institute of International Politics and Economics in Belgrade, published in *Danubius*,

no. 3/4, 1997, pp. 22–27)". However, at the time of completion of this book, the war in Kosovo is almost over, and thousands of people have already lost their lives.

7 Policy Issues

International war crimes tribunals, apart from representing a desire to institute impartial justice where otherwise moral chaos would rule, are also fundamentally a form of international intervention in a civil or regional conflict between national groups or states.

It is generally accepted in literature that, in deciding to intervene in a conflict area, the "international community" seeks to fulfil one or more of the following three main goals:

(1) To prevent a conflict,
(2) To manage a conflict where one has already occurred, and/or
(3) To resolve an ongoing conflict.

International war crimes tribunals are mainly an attempt to achieve the third goal. Their political mission, therefore, must take into account the political aspects of the situation on the ground, and their top criterion of success must be their effectiveness in reconciling the *political* conflict between nations, states or groups that supposedly *motivated* the actual armed conflict in the first place.

There are two main dimensions to the war crimes tribunals' work that facilitate the achievement of reconciliation. The *first* one is shifting the blame from entire nations to guilty individuals by bringing those guilty of war crimes to justice. The *second* dimension is impeccable *impartiality*. To balance these two aspects of the tribunals' work is the most difficult part of their job. It is exactly in the area of impartiality that the goal of reconciliation may be lost, for war crimes tribunals need not only *be* impartial, they must also be *seen as* impartial. The management of *perceptions* of war crimes tribunals requires the implementation of a number of other forms of international intervention in an internal or regional conflict.

The issue of shifting the blame for wartime atrocities from the entire nation or group to the individuals who actually committed the crimes is the more theoretical aspect of the tribunals' work.

The issue of impartiality is more practical. These two groups of problems therefore need to be addressed separately.

Shaping mutual perceptions

In situations where civil war between various national groups occurs, there are at least three groups of structural factors of internal conflict:

(1) Weak state structures,
(2) Internal security problems, and
(3) Complex and highly interwoven ethnic geography.[1]

In states with weak state structures ethnic conflict is more likely, because any security problems arising from factors (2) and (3) (such as potentially threatening inter-ethnic relations and tensions) are aggravated by the absence of effective state mechanisms for conflict-prevention and management. For example, where ethnic groups feel threatened by other groups, for whatever reason, and where the army is ineffective and divided along ethnic lines, where state authority is eroded, the police corrupt, the national groups will fall into the trap of the so-called "*security dilemma*". Because they assume that the other group will attack them, they conduct military training and defense development operations. This, when seen by the other groups, is interpreted as preparations for an assault, so the other groups start their own independent preparations. When the first group sees this as a confirmation of its fears, it accelerates the building of its army, so do the other groups, and tensions spiral until any spark of extremism from either side provokes an actual clash. *The security dilemma usually precedes civil wars.*

Assuming weak state structures, internal security problems, and critical ethnic geography, that is, the presence of all three structural factors of internal conflict (to a large extent, these are also the structural factors of many regional inter-state conflicts), *whether the security dilemma will occur or not depends primarily on mutual perceptions of the critical groups.* These perceptions, in turn, depend on how the other groups are portrayed by national elites. If the television and leading politicians of one group deliberately vilify the other group and engage in hate mongering, such as they did in the tragic conflict in Rwanda, then the security dilemma is highly likely. If, on the other hand, effort is placed in "balancing out" the perceptions, peace is more manageable. In such situations, national and/or group elites bear the primary responsibility for the occurrence of an armed conflict. Once the war starts, the populations may not be innocent and, strictly speaking, there may be room for considerable ascriptions of collective guilt, but the elites and critical individuals will always be the ones who are the most responsible for shaping mutual perceptions and thus also inciting or calming down the aggressive tensions. In other words, *the elites are usually the ones who could prevent the war.* This is the main practical reason why international intervention, including judicial intervention, always ought to concentrate on the assumption of individual, rather than collective guilt, with the aim of conflict-resolution in mind.

Responsibility for policy-design

Most war crimes occur as parts of an organized campaign. While the issue of individual responsibility for the operational aspects of war time atrocities is the most immediate one to be addressed by international war crimes courts, there remains an issue of responsibility of political oligarchies for policy-design of campaigns within which crimes had taken place.

The responsibility of politicians is usually the hardest to prove, because they can often claim ignorance of particular actions of operational field commanders and troops. However, the difficulty of proving "political guilt" for war crimes is often exaggerated by the external powers that stand behind the international intervention. Again the Croatian establishment has been a paradigmatic example of this.

The concept of criminal fault arising from spreading misinformation with an aim of inciting national, racial or religious hatred is well established in many a national criminal legislation. There is no reason why this concept should not be taken over and firmly applied by international judicial institutions. The principle of criminal responsibility arising from spreading hatred that has actually led to war could thus be applied.

Impartiality

There are rarely equally many war criminals on all sides in any conflict, and especially in civil wars. One side always has the upper hand, or has committed more atrocities than the other sides. The numbers of indictments for war crimes will therefore be higher for one side than for the others. This inevitably creates the perception that one side, that is, the whole nation or group, is guiltier than the other sides. As a result, inter-group antagonisms may escalate rather than be calmed down.

The perception of unequal guilt notwithstanding, clearly all those guilty of war crimes must be brought to answer for their actions, from whatever group they may be coming. However, the modalities of doing so must be maximally tuned to facilitate a de-escalation of inter-group tensions and bring about reconciliation. There are two radically different types of strategies for achieving the impression of impartiality by international war crimes tribunals, and consequently also by the international intervenors under whose auspices such tribunals are established and operate.

The "initial proportion" strategy

First, the courts and the foreign powers that back them can adopt the strategy of *initial proportion* between indictments. This means that, in the initial phase of the judicial intervention, the court takes care to balance out the cases it starts to try between the various nations or groups that have taken part in the war, and that need to be reconciled as part of the tribunal's mission. The initial proportion, while seemingly subduing the demands of truth and justice to those of politics, may not really be such a vicious approach. While balancing out the accusations initially helps establish the tribunal's credibility among the population at large that might be poorly informed about the real extent of crimes committed by "their own" perpetrators, it by no means grants any type of abolition to those who, because of the proportional approach, are not immediately indicted. It should be noted that the main task for international courts in this initial phase is to win support from the ordinary people on all sides. Although it is true that many ordinary people in a situation such as civil war rather fanatically support their own "heroes", many are also under pressure from local war lords and aggressive minorities within their own ranks. Many would like to see justice done, but not to a "historical detriment" of their own nation or group, which they fear could be the case if a partial international court dispenses justice. Winning over these people is the key requirement for international war crimes tribunals, both because they are the ones who will ultimately legitimize or delegitimize any new governments in the territories ravaged by war, but also because they will be the core of the civil society that is to emerge after the war. That civil society will need to trust the international organizations and be eager to reintegrate into the international community in the interest of global cooperation and lasting security in their region.

No one serious in any such national group really believes that there are equally many perpetrators of atrocities in all warring groups, but it helps them to be reassured about an international tribunal's impartiality when they see that initially there is a quantitatively "equal" approach to all parties in conflict.

To maximize the political effect of the initial proportion approach, the first indictments should be brought forward against the most notorious killers from all sides, *not* by the "*bottom-up*" strategy, starting from the immediate executors among the paratroopers and militia members. Every national group knows more or less precisely who the most notorious killers among their ranks are, and bringing those to justice first would maximize the perception of the tribunal as knowing exactly what it is doing. All others would then be called to answer for their deeds later on, after the tribunal has established a strong local credibility. This initial phase would last between one and three years, depending on local circumstances.

The massive imposition strategy

The second strategy for establishing credibility of international judicial intervention, radically different from the first one, is the *massive imposition* strategy. It means bringing in a large contingent of international troops, giving them a mandate to arrest all those suspected of having perpetrated atrocities, and trying all those arrested regardless of their nationality or group affiliation, and regardless of the political aspects of any perception of partiality that might be created among the population in this way.

While the initial proportion strategy emphasizes the initial perception of impartiality of the tribunal, the massive imposition strategy must compensate for an initial adversity, stemming from the local perception of its partiality, by a massive presence of force. The latter strategy emphasizes the later phase of the Tribunal's operation, when, in the course of five or more years, it will become clear that the pursuit of all war criminals is motivated only by a desire to fulfil justice and penalize all those who have violated the international humanitarian law.

The ICTY has slowly adopted the massive imposition strategy since 1996, although in a modified version. In this modified version, a large part of the pressure applied on the sides in conflict to force them to cooperate with the Tribunal has come from international political measures, conditioning of foreign aid, and restrictions on the concerned countries' participation in international organizations.

This strategy involves substantial commitments of resources and political credibility at home. It also involves one or a few dominant military and economic powers contributing most of the practical means for executing the strategy, while the basis of legitimization of such actions lies with large international organizations, most typically the UN. International troops thus find themselves in an array of occupiers' roles: from arresting local officials and dignitaries to holding or supervising elections, shutting down radio and television stations, even entering into open confrontation with the local army and police. This is not a democratic role for any international organization or force, and should be avoided at all cost, because it brings up the darkest memories of times of international aggression and domination.

The massive imposition strategy has one major advantage over the initial proportion strategy: it is operationally simple, because it is similar to occupation. The well-tried recipes for successful (and unsuccessful) invasions and occupations apply here. The local idiosyncrasies are mostly placed under control, the rules of the game imposed from the outside. A whole range of political questions relating to delivering the accused to the international court, relationship between the judicial action and other aspects of an essentially political international intervention in the conflict, become largely irrelevant. The massive imposition strategy does not depend for its effectiveness on how cooperative the locals will be — they have no choice but to cooperate. In essence, this is a strategy that is contrary to international law and accepted norms of conduct of international relations.

As with all seemingly simple solutions, this one, too, is often of little real value. From the point of view of the occupiers, it is an ideal scenario for international interventions. The massive imposition strategy as an American ideal has been discernible in the often quoted criteria for the involvement of US troops in crisis areas that were adopted by the highest Pentagon officials after the "Desert Storm" operation against Iraq. These criteria include:

(i)   Clear definition of national interests and terms of the mission,
(ii) Clear chain of command,
(iii) Deployment of overwhelming force for the task in order to minimize the casualties in the intervening force, and
(iv) A clear exit strategy.

In most situations, this is simply impossible, especially when an international, multilateral military intervention is linked with securing the operational viability of an international war crimes tribunal.

There are several major shortcomings of the massive imposition strategy.

First, only a few conflicts will allow such a large mobilization of national resources in any "democratic" country that is supposed to execute the bulk of the intervention.

Second, multi-national cooperation between the intervenors is so much more difficult where the anticipated commitment of each one's resources is greater. This makes multi-national action, and thus also the legitimization of intervention within the large international organizations, more complex.

Third, even if all other aforementioned criteria are fulfilled, and multi-national action executed, in most interventions in internal conflicts the last criterion, a clear exit strategy, will be difficult to fulfill, because it is impossible to say what amount of time it will take for the initial phase of possible distrust towards the intervenors and their institutions by the locals to pass, and for belief in the "impartiality" of the pursuit of the guilty by the intervenors to develop and become firmly established. It is therefore also difficult to anticipate the period of commitment of troops, the amount of resources needed, and the success of the aggression in the short-to-medium term. Apart from being criminal in nature, this is also a highly dangerous strategy for the entire international order.

In other words, the massive intervention strategy is potentially a bottomless pit that could turn into an intervention nightmare for the intervenors. It is therefore a highly risky, politically very difficult type of strategy overall. The relevant dimensions of the massive intervention strategy correspond to Picture1.

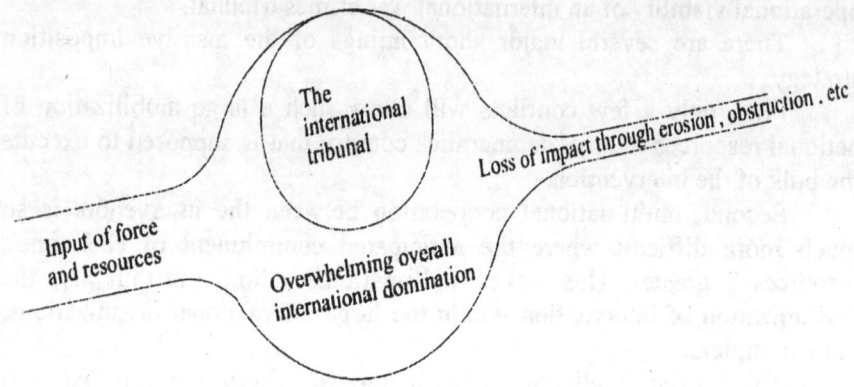

Picture 1: The "balloon" of the massive imposition strategy

The balloon of intervention may "blow out" if troops pull out, and if that happens in the short-to-medium term, the international court disappears along with the massive intervention effort.

The initial proportion strategy, on the other hand, is presented by Picture 2. It requires a moderate commitment of resources, symbolized by a tube as opposed to a balloon, where the court for war crimes must accommodate itself to limiting circumstances (symbolized by its being "squeezed" into an ellipse, as opposed to being comfortably accommodated in a perfect circle), but the strategy gradually creates local support and more room for the court to maneuver (symbolized by the widening of the tube without the prospect of a "blow-out" that could threaten the court itself).

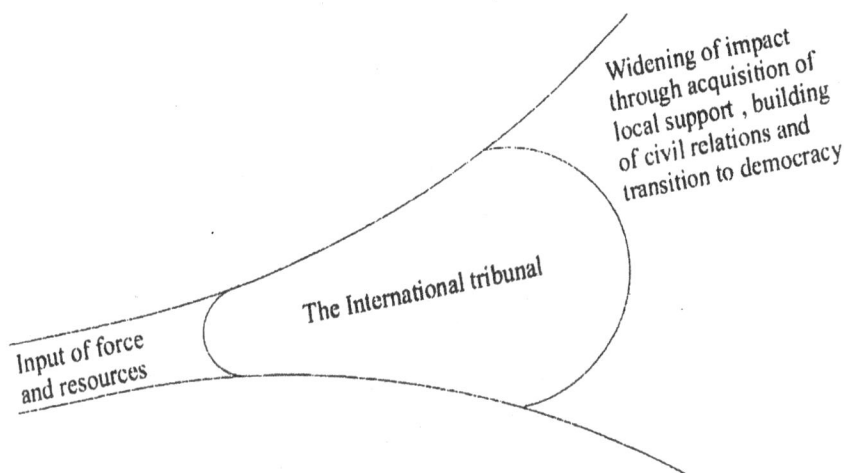

Picture 2: The "tube" of the initial proportion strategy

The initial proportion strategy, although seemingly controversial from a strictly judicial point of view, is by far strategically superior and more likely to eventually result in all those suspected of war time atrocities being brought to justice than is the massive imposition strategy. The former strategy is also the one that is more likely to produce the impression of impartiality in the short-to-medium term, which is crucial for the sustainability and political feasibility of the entire work of any international court.

Note

.1 See Brown, M.E. (ed.), *The international dimensions of internal conflict*, MIT Press, Cambridge, Mass., 1996, pp. 1–32.

8 NATO and the ICTY

On 20 March 1947, Jan Masaryk, the then Czechoslovak Foreign Minister, held a parliamentary speech envisioning the role of Czechoslovakia in the future new Europe by the following words:

> Neither a curtain, nor a bridge, but a democratic chain that encompasses the world and holds this planet of Earth together.

In his notes for the publication of the same speech, Masaryk added:

> I would advise everyone who contemplates the problems of our foreign policy to do it with a map in their hands. Many people are almost hypnotized by the press, radio and in all other manner, so that it appears that there are already two worlds today — the western, and the eastern one. So we have become western and eastern in social gatherings, in our offices and in our families. This is an unhealthy thing — especially for our small nation. Anyone can see on the map that the world has four sides, and that, apart from the West and East, there are also the North and South.

Masaryk would have hardly contemplated the break-up of the former Yugoslavia in the bloody way in which it occurred, nor would he have liked to envision the role NATO has had to play to bring an end to the bloodshed in the Balkans in the 1990s. This was partly because Masaryk's times were ones of disenchantment, but also of idealism with the newly found European peace. Partly this is also because Masaryk was a central European.

Politics in southeastern Europe, and particularly the policies of the Yugoslav states towards the ICTY, have been considerably influenced by the role NATO has played in the region, especially concerning the plans for a continued expansion of the Alliance into eastern Europe. The issues of Balkan security are somewhat more complicated than those of the rest of Europe, because of long-lasting and structurally very complicated ethnic, cultural, military, and, of course, international political interests in the Balkans. The civil wars in the former Yugoslavia were largely an expression of different forms of ethnic and ethno-political heritage, sometimes highly determined by ethno-political violence. Today's outlooks of the Balkan states, especially those that have been established on the territory of the former Yugoslavia, regarding an eventual future integration with NATO, the relevance, and influence of NATO expansion in eastern Europe, are considerably different. One should therefore not underestimate the potential of NATO expansion policy to impact on relations among Balkan states, as well as between them and the rest of Europe. The issue of expansion is to be taken as a vital dilemma for future Balkan security, and, as the 1999 Kosovo crisis has shown, NATO's actions in the region may determine the direction the development of the region's relations with the ICTY will take. A brief discussion of the politics of NATO in the region thus seems appropriate.

NATO in the Balkans

A traditional line of argument against NATO expansion is based on the "unpaid bills" theory, namely on unresolved conflicts or potential conflicts between the candidates for membership in the Alliance. During discussions about the possible acceptance of Hungary into NATO, the relationship between Hungary and Romania was a controversial issue. The relations between the two states were at one stage under particular pressure, because of ethno-political problems arising from the two million strong Hungarian national minority issues in the Romanian region of Transylvania. At the time, there were arguments that Hungary and Romania should join together, because any other solution could disturb the equilibrium in their mutual military relations. If only one country were invited to join the Alliance, it was argued, that country could then attempt to use its critical advantage to "resolve" ethno-political issues by force. In such a chance-taking scheme of action, the security of NATO members would be directly threatened, and they could be dragged into a chronic conflict in eastern Europe over an issue of at best marginal importance to almost all of them.

The key point here is why the threat has in fact not occurred. Hungary was eventually invited to join the Alliance in the "first wave of expansion", while Romania remained out in the cold for the time being. The political reactions in Romania were extremely tumultuous, and even the subsequent 1997 visit of US President Clinton to Bucharest was carried out under conditions of high risk. The situation satisfied all conditions for a security dilemma, yet the scenario of a security dilemma did not occur. A probable explanation is to be found in the fact that the integration of Hungary into NATO is being carried out in the conditions of both domestic and foreign policy stability of both Hungary and Romania, without recent military conflicts between the two countries, and with moderate mutual policies of the two governments. It is probably true that these political circumstances play the role of a powerful antidote to potential security dilemmas more generally.[1] However, if serious consideration was given to the integration of some Balkan states into NATO with others being left outside, the consequences could well be entirely different, exactly because the antidote political circumstances do not apply to these states. Balkan countries have tense mutual relations, a very recent history of mutual warfare, most are politically unstable from the inside (some more, like FRY, and some less, like Bulgaria), and highly politically vulnerable in foreign policy matters. They are all highly dependant on foreign political and economic support, and they are in a process of consolidation of their roles in the immensely powerful large international organizations, some of which have a direct influence on the pending resolutions of Balkan regional affairs (such as the UN, OSCE, and, to some extent, the Council of Europe).

In the course of NATO's intervention over Kosovo in 1999, the international circles voiced plans for a "Stability Pact" for southeastern Europe, which would not only help compensate all the countries affected by the bombing for the economic and infrastructural losses incurred, but also strive to integrate them into the EU and NATO structures through a fast track procedure. This is a controversial issue in the region. Some Balkan analysts, like Radovan Vukadinović, advocate the extension of NATO's military guarantees to the Balkans. According to this view, in extending its membership to the Balkans NATO should use the principle of *selective* acceptance of those states that fulfill certain pre-set political and military criteria. Vukadinović argues that, according to those criteria, Croatia should be allowed to join. This, then, would introduce a healthy competition among the Balkan states for the fulfillment of the criteria leading up to NATO membership. According to Vukadinović, they would compete to democratize as soon as possible, and to achieve international standards in a range of domestic policy areas. All this would be motivated by security reasons, that is, by the wish or each country in the region to join NATO as well as the Significant Other Balkan state, with which there might be a bilateral issue that causes tension in mutual relations. In such a way, according to Vukadinović, the *de facto* degree of cohesion between the former Yugoslav states would increase, or, more precisely, their mutual suspicions would lead up to them behaving themselves better in order not to be left out of NATO. This, in turn, would diminish the potential for new wars or a breakout of political violence through terrorism and guerrilla warfare.[2] In other words, this is the rationale behind the thoughts about a "Stability Pact".

To be precise, in his analysis Vukadinović sees the possibility of a reversal of the security dilemma, where giving a critical advantage to one regional state over the others would cause the others to improve their policies in order to neutralize the critical disadvantage that they are at, rather than engage in a destructive military build-up and defense postures that could provoke actual violence. This, of course, is one possibility. It seems, however, that the theory does not sufficiently take into account the other possibility, namely that states may react differently, motivated by scenarios where they expect or receive support from quarters other than NATO, by internal instability, by the need to accommodate radicals in the area of domestic policy, etc. The crisis with Yugoslavia resisting NATO for seventy odd days, defying the military odds, demonstrated at least the possibility of a different reaction.

On the one hand, encompassing the Balkans in the process of NATO expansion is a strategically logical step for NATO, as the opposite would entail a discontinuity in the European territory controlled by the Alliance towards the East and the Russian borders. It is in the strategic interest of NATO to increase the territorial, geo-strategic and operational homogeneity of Europe under its control, in order to maximize its military potential in regard to any regional crisis. In this scenario, the integration of the Balkans is desirable. However, even if the desirability of Balkan integration into NATO is granted at this point, it remains highly controversial whether the dynamics of their mutual relations, and their bilateral relations with NATO, would unfold according to what Vukadinovi pictures as a reverse security dilemma scenario.

Thus, on the other hand, a serious consideration of the integration of former Yugoslav states into NATO leads to at least two types of problems. The first one is related to mutually considerably different "NATO policies" of particular Balkan states. For example, FR Yugoslavia is not a member of Partnership for Peace and is not showing any intent to seek NATO membership in the near future. On the contrary, the rump Yugoslav federal authorities consider NATO as a threat to their interests. The verbally quoted reasons for this include NATO's open engagement on the side of Muslim and Croatian forces against the Serbian troops in Bosnia, which was the turning point in the Bosnian war, with the Bosnian Serb Army suffering its first major defeats and territorial losses on the ground, leading up to the eventual conclusion of the Dayton-Paris Peace Accords. Finally, after the NATO–FRY war of 1999, NATO is pictured as an aggressor and an open strategic adversary.

The second type of problem is operational, i.e. it relates to a grave lack of operational conditions for the acceptance of Balkan states into the Alliance. The mutual relations between these countries are hostile and highly irrationally charged. Even the smallest escalation in the numerous regional foci of conflict may be sufficient to trigger the latent mutual warfare that has marked relations between those countries for almost a decade since the onset of the civil wars in the former Yugoslavia in 1990-1991.

To be quite precise, there is an extremely high probability that a selective NATO expansion into the Balkans at this stage might trigger a fully-fledged security dilemma, not in the reversed form, but in the "straight", destructive and potentially fatal form. The "antidote" conditions of internal and external political stability do not apply in the Balkans. The manipulation of highly irrational animosities by malignant ethnic and political elites has demonstrated its deadly potential during the most severe bloodletting on the Continent since the Second World War. The "accounts" opened by the mass crimes in the war have not been settled. The ICTY has been relatively unsuccessful so far in bringing justice to bear upon the perpetrators.

Even if the consequences of the war with NATO in 1999 were forgotten, and if all former Yugoslav states were to opt for joining NATO unanimously, their quest for an early NATO membership would more likely take the form of an armaments race and mutual obstruction, in order to achieve the critical advantage for early integration. The "straight" security dilemma would be a much more likely outcome in any case than the "reverse", constructive and cooperative form of the security dilemma.

Even if NATO were to find a way to integrate all former Yugoslav states at once, without generating a security dilemma, which would be extremely difficult, such a group of new members would undoubtedly bring major instability to the Alliance. They could make the decision-making processes more difficult through mutual policy-confrontations and competitive strategic considerations inherited from their pre-NATO history. They could thus jeopardize not only the organizational cohesion, but also the operational efficiency of NATO troops in the eastern European theatre and elsewhere in the world.

The high political quarters inside NATO often stress that the new mission of NATO in Europe is to control low-intensity armed conflicts, regional in nature, and with a high, if not predominant, degree of *ethno-*

political motivation. If this is truly regarded as the main reason for a planned further NATO expansion into eastern Europe, where it is supposed to fill the "security vacuum" created by the withdrawal of the Soviet armies formerly acting under the legitimization umbrella of the Warsaw Treaty, then any inclusion of countries that could threaten the very ability of NATO to fulfill that mission, in the operational sense, would have to be out of the question.

Arguably, a further NATO expansion into eastern Europe would not be in the security interests of the three central European countries invited to join the Alliance at the NATO "supersummit" in Madrid, in June 1997 (Poland, Hungary and the Czech Republic). Such a further expansion could place the new NATO members in a direct line of fire from Russia, not because of any escalation of relations with Russia, but paradoxically, along with the diplomatic warming of relations with the Kremlin. This would be mostly due to changes in the objective defense constellation in Europe, especially regarding Russia's defense capabilities and doctrines. These changes may demand modifications in the Russian defense doctrines and strategy to the detriment of potential security of central Europe, due to its inclusion in NATO.

Furthermore, the enlargement of NATO may well not be in the interest of the Balkan states either, especially Yugoslavia, because it could generate an unhealthy military competition and an arms race, thus further worsening the region's security crisis. Such an expansion could also paralyze NATO as the major intervention force in the region, contributing systematically to its security through its role as an intervenor, with the possible new Balkan NATO members' mutual differences acting to block NATO decision-making and coordination.

Neither is a further expansion in the interest of Russia. It would represent a direct threat to Russia's security logic, and would require a more aggressive Russian defense posture towards the West, an increase in expenditures for military needs, and a reorganization of the Russian armies to put them on a higher level of combat-readiness in facing the armies of the enlarged NATO on the Russian frontiers.

Finally, a further expansion would not be in the interest of NATO itself, as it would effectively charge the Alliance with comprehensive conflict-management tasks in a region where it is insufficiently familiar with the social, military, and even political relations. NATO could find itself dragged into long-lasting guerrilla warfare, and where its members could face the dangers of internal political crises. On the other hand, NATO's application of overwhelming force to manage regional conflicts would considerably reduce the possibility of prolonged guerilla wars, but such a strategy would impose such costs on NATO members that the costs themselves could cause political problems inside the Alliance. A further expansion would proportionally reduce NATO's cohesion and efficiency. The growing plurality of interests inside NATO could induce confusion, internal conflicts and, possibly, paralyze the decision-making systems.

Learning to soothe the sores: European cultures within NATO

The above conclusions are mostly based on considerations of military strategy in eastern Europe. However, this perspective by no means excludes other security issues that are non-military in nature. For example, the internal political violence that has dramatically increased in the "rump" Yugoslavia over the past decade is a major security threat that cannot be resolved by military means.

The application of force against FRY in 1999 has demonstrated that NATO's aggressive policy in the region can destabilize relations between states and initiate a reconfiguration of loyalties and security mechanisms that threaten the region's peace. The role NATO will play in the region will depend on what part of its culture it decides to pronounce. The more moderate culture of NATO's European members, in the context of the Alliance's actions being appropriately subordinated to the UN Security Council, might be able to act as an antidote for Balkan feuding, but the more aggressive culture of the US could be the oil that, when added to the fire of the existing confrontations, may cause the region to go up in flames.

Balkan radicalism

In his manuscript that, according to Czech President and long time anticommunist dissident Vaclav Havel, founded the European concept of foreign policy, Jiri Dinstbier, Foreign Minister of the divorced Czech Republic, wrote about Europe:

> Europe has the experience of a common existence of various societies. These societies have always had to seek their own identity not on their own, but through the interaction of various groups that lived in close proximity. Of course, the impulse for change can also come from European traditions of America and Russia, but the experience of interaction of small European

communities is indispensable. Both giants are faced with the obstacle to understand it, due to their weight and dimensions, which make it possible for the tension to weaken in space. In the case of Russia, there are remainders of the oriental despotic rule, and in America the tradition of the individual American dream and the concept of the melting pot which, actually, confirms the sovereignty of an individual, but dissolves the individualism of various communities (...) In (a European's) experience, the freedom of an individual has a larger, deeper, and more bitter content than for an American. Respect for the neighbor as an individual is also respect for his specificity (to be different from the others is a crime, said one American author), of his personal, but also linguistic, group, national, ideological specificity, of his social belonging. A European presupposes these differences as creative elements of a pluralist European society.[3]

Dinstbier here nicely contrasts the European ideal of moderation and tolerance, systematically fostered within the European Communities since their inception, with the more extreme political cultures of the former superpowers. In the late 1990s, unfortunately, a similar contrast can be drawn between the moderate cultures of western Europe and the hard-core phenomenon of political and societal radicalism in the successor states of the former Yugoslavia.

The former Yugoslav republics have in fact been largely products of the new constellation of relations in southeastern Europe, with national elites usurping an increasing slice of power and control, and nationalism becoming the dominant ideology in all the successor states. It was nationalism that drove the secessionist tendencies in Slovenia, Croatia and Bosnia and Herzegovina. It was also nationalism that determined the policies of the successor states at all times when issues of state interest were at stake.

Nationalism in the successor states rests on a deep divide between the ruling elites and the population. Nationalist tendencies are shaped and served by the elite, and passively followed by the citizens, at least by the majority of those who condone what the government does. Radicalism in thought and action is closely connected with the radical consequences it yields, for at one stage it becomes unclear whether the radical state of affairs in the society was caused by the government's radical policies, or radical policies are the only conceivable sort of responses to such escalated societal circumstances.[4]

Political moderation has been a major cause of stability in western Europe since the Second World War. Such moderation involved readiness to seek common interests and integrative incentives rather than insist on mutual differences and contradictions. Generally, most forms of political coexistence, be they federations of states or cooperative regional agreements, are based on the tacit assumption that policy-preference will be given to common and constructive elements, and that extreme, radical and exclusivist views will either be suppressed, or, if they are an element of the public agenda, that they will be put on a political back-burner. This is especially true of troublesome and hectic times through which most federations and regions marked by long-term stability have gone on occasions.

The range of policy-options available to any given national elite or state authority on any given occasion is quite broad: from seeking to calm down the tensions within society, to deliberately inciting blood-letting, with a view of advancing bizarre strategies for the internal consolidation of power. The choice of means goes with the choice of policies — moderate policies generally involve moderate means, while extreme policies require extreme means. The recent history of western Europe has shown a democratic tradition of moderation in the choice of means and the choice of policies that has brought a good deal of stability and prosperity to the participating nations, and the gradual realization of the ideal of "the United States of Europe" that was once looked upon as a dream by the handful of people labeled "European idealists".

There have, of course, been exceptions to the moderate style of political management of western Europe over the past fifty years, but these exceptions have been successfully absorbed by a democratic culture arising from the set of values advanced by leaders who deliberately engaged in moderate manners of governance. Exactly owing to such culture, the issue of internal consolidation and maintenance of power and the issue of moderation, security and continuity not only of foreign and domestic policy, but also of the very manner of governance, have become closely connected in the minds of the European citizens.

Democratic societies are less prone to radicalization, and issues of stability and good neighborly relations in western Europe witness the constructive potential of politically moderate agendas. Moderate political means dominate the policy agendas of all EU member countries. There are policies that breach universally accepted standards of human rights (such as those relating to the treatment and deportation of refugees in Germany), or policies that seriously question the importance of European consensus in security affairs and the rule of international law (such as the British participation, with the US, in the 1999 bombing of Iraq, and even more pronounced, in the bombing of FRY in 1999. However, all-in-all, extreme and radical policies in the democratic western European countries occur relatively rarely.

Generally speaking, there are three main features accompanying radical policies in democratic states.[5]

1. First, radical policies in democracies are typically used to address a burning issue for the political elite when no other means are available. The crisis with the large influx of refugees into Germany after the onset of the Yugoslav civil war was one example. The crisis arising from Mr. Clinton's scandalous conduct in the Monica Lewinsky affair and the importance of keeping good relations between London and Washington probably led Britain to participate in shedding carpets of bombs over Baghdad at the very end of 1998. These are extreme policies undertaken in desperation, caused by mistakes in an otherwise moderate climate of political management.
2. Secondly, in order to be sustainable by the population and the political system, extreme measures need to be by far offset by the "good deeds". In democratic systems such moves are politically expensive. To be banal, the expulsion of refugees costs a great deal of clout among the immigrant voters at the next election, which the now former German Chancellor Helmut Kohl may or may not be aware of, and the sustainability of an indecent presidential affair in the Oval Office eats all the credit from several years of good economic and employment policy.
3. Thirdly, because of what was said under (2), politicians involved in extreme or discrediting actions, if they politically survive, tend to behave themselves afterwards, as the price they would have paid by then is devastating. It is unlikely that the German Government will expel any more refugees *en masse*, until the next election, and one would hope that Mr. Clinton would now try to refrain from illicit liaisons and wake-up bombings for some time at least.

In a recent paper, Rastko Močnik points out to the emergence of a new ideology in the Balkans.[6] He calls this ideology "Balkanism" and defines it as one of double domination. One form of domination is that of the paradigm of "cooperative, civilized Europe" over the internally accepted stereotype of "the uncooperative, violent and backward Balkans" and the functioning of this submission as a means of the Balkans' integration into the European integrative systems. The other form of domination is the internal, violent and oppressive one, employed by Balkan regimes over the citizens. In such societies, radicalism functions quite differently from the way it works in democratic societies with a tradition of moderation. Among other characteristics, radical policies satisfy the following important three:

1. Radical policies do not only serve as an emergency measure to address a burning issue. They are a style of governance. Given the unstable state of affairs in societies in this part of the world, radical policies tend to be accepted as more or less normal, even as "the only possible" norm of governance.
2. Radicalism is a factor of stability, rather than instability, in the sense that governments do not lose office because of radical policies — as the example of the former Yugoslav states shows, the political establishments in this part of the world have developed an amazing ability to use radical policies and the devastating consequences arising from them, including major military defeats and territorial losses, to further consolidate their internal power structures and hold on the populations, rather than incurring any damages to their control.
3. Radicalism is in no way limited to political forces that are usually conceptually identified with right-wing policies. Many political formations that are nominally describable as being "left" have quite right-wing agendas. The Social-Democratic Party in the southern Yugoslav republic of Montenegro is more right wing than any other party, and as part of the three-party coalition (with the People's Party and the Democratic Party of Socialists — former communists) it advocates Montenegrin nationalism, secession from FR Yugoslavia and the development of independent foreign policy.

Part of the reason for all this is that it is somewhat of a misnomer to speak of "security crises" in the former Yugoslavia as the most problematic part of the Balkans today. There are probably no real security crises arising from radical polices, like there are in the West. That may be the main intricacy. Instead, there is rather a continuous *policy of insecurity* as a mechanism for the maintenance of political power that is based on pursuing a *deliberate* and more or less *controlled implosion of the system*.

The "policy of implosion" involves the following mechanism: The government, or national elite, first escalate an internal controversy with external consequences in order to create a smoke-screen for corruption and abuse of the system that they themselves commit. An example is blowing a national issue out of every proportion until external, foreign attention is sufficiently attracted to come to bear upon the domestic conflict. After some time, the regime gives up on the controversial (such as ethnic) issue, under international pressure. It sacrifices that it has up to that point deemed a vital national interest, in exchange for favors that are then used to consolidate the existing power structures in an impoverished (or territorially reduced) land. The system, the society, the state, thus continually implode and weaken, while the ruling structure grows ever stronger in the weakened system. In the end, the society is so poor and fragile, and the government in it so strong, that the society can hardly be distinguished from the government. Alternatives to the government are either non-existent, or negligible in influence.

The implosion involves two parallel currents:

(a) First, it involves an external alienation of all parts of society that may represent a threat to the conservative core of the system, and that might represent the destructive consequences of the regime's behavior in their true light.
(b) The second current involves an internal consolidation of power through national homogenization, by the mechanisms of fear, intimidation and isolation, not shying away from open coercion over the voters.

In this manner, the population is cut-off from real levers of power. Through intimidation, exploitation of the state-controlled media, and imposition of radical reasoning and radical policies, the population has been driven to a stage where it perceives the government as a natural disaster that has to be survived. As a consequence, the population has largely lost political consciousness. The security crisis in the Balkans is therefore not that — a crisis. It is a policy of insecurity that will invariably lead to a further fragmentation of the region, where intervention in the crisis is linked with the removal of sources of radical policies from power. This cannot be done through pressure on the population, but on the national elites directly.

In the democratic societies of western Europe, due to the moderate political climate, extremes remain just that — extremes, and appropriately receive the characterization of scandals. There are thus only so many scandals that any government in a democratic political system can take without being replaced. The fewer scandals, the more stability and continuity in the power quarters. And conversely, the more scandals, the less power, prestige and chance to retain the political office.

In the Balkans today, one witnesses quite the opposite. The radicalization of political life is a guarantor of continuation of political power, because continuous crises do not allow sufficient time and opportunity for viable political alternatives to emerge, or for a mature political process to run its course fully. Radicalization here takes different shapes. It is not limited to the former Yugoslavia. For example, the confrontational positions that many Balkan countries have adopted towards Russia under NATO's influence during the 1999 Kosovo crisis is a radical policy that is detrimental to southeastern European peace and stability. The blocking of Russia's efforts to assert its role in the peace-keeping mission in Kosovo by denying its troops the air corridors over Bulgaria, Romania and Hungary, under the influence of NATO, is a radical response by those governments that stands in contrasts with the tradition of moderate relations with Russia, and that exhibits a strong partiality and short-term opportunism of the three governments that might incur a heavy cost in terms of long term stability and good relations with Russia.

Reconciliation as a "switch" for radicalism

The radical policies that have dominated the agenda of disintegration of the former Yugoslavia have been fueled by self-perpetuating animosities crudely grouped under the term "nationalism". Yet, this nationalism has largely been a result of confusion caused by the cave-in of the ideological system that had been induced as the fundamental "glue" that kept together the former communist societies.

It is proving that, after antagonistic culminations reflected in civil wars, the torn apart civic institutions and practices cannot be simply revamped by international domination, occupation or dictate. What seems to be required is reconciliation and, trickily enough, reconciliation, like love, cannot be brought about by force or any type of pressure.

A part of the ICTY's mission has been to help bring about reconciliation by determining individual faults and leaving room open for the forgiveness of collective faults or those actions or inaction that may appear as faults. This strategy, as has been argued here, involves various sorts of pressure in order to be operationally viable. However, with the Kosovo crisis, this pressure reached an unprecedented level with NATO, not the UN, taking on the most pronounced role of a military enforcer engaged in a suppression of Serbian national interests in Kosovo. To make things even more complicated, this was not an enforcement of any decisions or acts of the ICTY or the UN as its umbrella organization, but of an independent political agenda designed by NATO-constituent governments, where the ICTY was incorporated *into* that independent political agenda by being allocated a role of exerting pressure on Serbia by bringing up charges against five of its top political and military leaders.

This is not to say that on this occasion the ICTY has acted *merely* as a political instrument of NATO — it is by no means excluded that it could have its own independent judicial reasons for becoming involved in the way in which it did. However, the fact that there was a political synergism between the ICTY and NATO in this instance, and that it was obvious, has changed the equation of reconciliation and pressure.

Namely, if the goal is, say, reconciliation, and if the instrument for achieving this goal is bringing forward an indictment, and an instrument for enforcing the indictment (making an arrest) is military pressure, say by NATO, authorized by the UN, that is one matter. However, if the goal is sought to be achieved by the Court becoming, or allowing to appear to be becoming integrated into a broader political and military agenda that in itself is independent of either the ICTY or the UN, then it is quite another matter. Assuming that the substance of the judicial rationale for the indictment is correct and justified, the two contexts or strategies render reconciliation as a method of "switching off" radicalism and violence quite different. Even if, from a strictly judicial point of view, the substance of the indictment is impeccable (which in the case of the indictment of Slobodan Milošević, Milan Milutinović, Nikola Šainović, Vlajko Stojiljković and Dragoljub Ojdanić is not the case, because the indictment is based *solely* on positional responsibility, rather than on *any* evidence of factual involvement or responsibility in particular instances), the peace-enabling dimension of it, which is an inalienable part of the Tribunal's work, is severely compromised in the latter constellation.

NATO, the UN, and the ICTY

Part of the problem sketched above is structural. The UN and NATO are two different organizations, with considerably different interests, procedures, policies and means available. The ICTY is part of the UN system. If it acts in any synergism with NATO when NATO acts in ways not sanctioned by the UN, organizational, legitimizational, and even legal controversies ensue. The other part of the problem is connected with the principle of subordination that is applicable. If the UN is conceived as the supreme global legitimizing body for coercive actions against any of its member states, and the ICTY as an organ of all of the UN member states for prosecuting war crimes in the former Yugoslavia, then one group of the member states (NATO members) acting contrary to the opinion of at least some of the other member states (such as Russia, China, or India), against another member state, without a mandate by the UN governing body in matters of security, may not involve the ICTY or else the system of the UN is brought in jeopardy. These are procedural issues, and procedure is often less than sufficiently well suited to the demands and constraints of reality, but important issues nevertheless they are that may not be ignored.

In Kosovo, NATO appears to play the initiating, the enablement and the controlling role for the ICTY. It plays the initiating role by first starting the war and then handing over evidence and proposals for indictments to the ICTY that were clearly biased (handed over and composed by a participant in and initiator of the war, and based on one-sided accounts and intelligence). These proposals, unlike those handed over the other side, were acted upon by the ICTY extremely rapidly and in an extremely politically opportune moment for NATO, by charging the top political and military brass of NATO's adversary at the height of the conflict.

NATO also plays the enabling role, because it is NATO that secures access for ICTY investigators and manages Kosovo while investigations take place.

Finally, NATO also plays the controlling role, because its political activity, including official statements by its leaders concerning possible indictments and judicial actions prejudice the ICTY's moves, and these moves at least appear to follow those political actions by NATO leaders. This is a situation that, at least perceivedly, bestows the three key roles concerning the ICTY upon NATO, instead of the UN, thus disturbing the principle of subordination or the political perception of it. While in theory the highest authority in matters like Kosovo is the Security Council, it has been almost entirely circumvented by NATO. While the ICTY is theoretically supposed to be independent even of the Security Council in its work, although it is organizationally subordinate to it, it appears to be integrated in the NATO diplomacy. Finally, while in theory the supreme rule of the UN in regional conflicts is based on the principle of predominantly consensual decisions on a maximally broad international scale, the self-superimposition of NATO upon the UN has generated deep international divides between key members of the Security Council. During the NATO–FRY war, these cleavages have at times threatened to change the entire system of post-Cold War international relations.

From these institutional controversies it is clear that the ICTY is not merely a court in the ordinary sense of the word, but that it is a highly sensitive and potent international body that can act for the good or for the bad of both peace and reconciliation in the former Yugoslavia, and of international order more broadly conceived.

Reconciliation as the antidote to Balkan radicalism is badly needed, and a more balanced and firmly steered course by the ICTY is crucial. The experience of the ICTY will play an important part in the work of the envisaged permanent International Criminal Tribunal in The Hague, and will thus play the role of a blueprint for international criminal justice. At the same time, the ICTY by its actions will largely determine the directions and pace of development or redevelopment of inter-communal bonds in the former Yugoslavia. Clear strategic vision, including the resolution of the controversies espoused here, and a firm institutional and systemic repositioning of the ICTY within the UN system seem as pre-requisites for a reform of the ICTY. The reform should address at least the issues touched upon in this book, and it should incorporate both a normative reform governing the ICTY's work within the UN system (addressing issues such as checks and control responsibilities, liabilities for miscarriages of justice and other aspects of a common sense normative framework for a fully accountable criminal court), and the institutional and political reform of the ICTY as a diplomatic instrument. The latter part of the reform would address the issues of returning an appropriate degree of independence to the ICTY and the complementary process of clarifying the diplomatic and general policy guidance priority and subordination of the ICTY to the United Nations and the Security Council.

What is at stake with the ICTY is the future of a blueprint of international criminal justice, as well as the issues of finally making decisive inroads into the process of putting the politics of antagonism in southeastern Europe behind.

Notes

1   The theory of security dilemmas is not the subject here, but the assumption would probably hold very well if tested in such a theory.

2   Vukadinović, R., "The enlargement of NATO and the countries of former Yugoslavia", *Peace and Security*, vol. XXIX, September 1997, pp. 13–23. I have presented a different opinion in Fatić, A., "Expansion in a ghastly light", *Peace and Security*, vol. XXX, March 1998, pp. 36–40.

3   Dinstbier, J., *Sanjarenje o Evropi (Dreaming of Europe)*, transl. from the Czech into Serbian by A. Ilić, Dečje novine, Gornji Milanovac, 1991., pp. 154–5.

4   Useful considerations of what could be considered radical developments in the government policies in FRY are espoused by Milan Popović in Popović, M., *Politički apartheid: Balkanska postmoderna 3 (Political apartheid: The Balkan Post-Moderna 3)*, Monitor, Podgorica, 1997. To explain the quasi-biological nature of the politics in the Balkans, Popović appropriately uses the phrase "survival of the fittest" — Ibid., p. 56. Another brilliant account of radicalism in the Balkans is that by Ivan Iveković, in an article entitled "Neopatrijarhat i političko nasilje: Prilog razumevanju etničkih sukoba na Balkanu i Kavkazu" ("Neo-patriarchat and political violence: Contribution to a better understanding of the ethnic conflicts in the Balkans and the Caucasus"), published in *Republika*, Belgrade, no. 174, 1997, pp. I–XX. Iveković's main thesis is that radicalism and political violence can be explained by the conflict between a dying agrarian and an emerging industrial era ("(...) what we are witnessing are the ferocious convulsions of a traumatized agrarian society, destined to perish, and the equally hard birth pains of an industrial order in the making. (...) Social unrest and political violence have always marked the transition from one cycle to the other. This time, the escalated social tensions have taken the form of an ethnic conflict, thus hiding underneath the deeper societal contradictions." — Ibid., p. XX).

5   Although it was said that *societal radicalization* is less likely in democratic than in autocratic societies, it should be quite clear here that *radical policies* are by no means the exclusive property of non-democratic systems — they regularly occur in "western", "democratic" societies.

6   Močnik, R., "The Balkans as a stereotype", unpublished manuscript.

Bibliography

"A future security agenda for Europe: Report of the Independent Working Group established by the Stockholm International Peace Research Institute", *European Security*, vol. 6, no. 2, Summer 1997.

Alison, M., "US ready to keep a force in Bosnia 18 months longer," *New York Times*, 11 November 1996, p. 1.

Arend, A.C. & Beck, R.J., *International law and the use of force* Routledge, London, 1993.

Arms Project for Human Rights Watch and Physicians for Human Rights, *Landmines: A deadly legacy*, Human Rights Watch and Physicians for Human Rights, Washington, 1993.

Aya, R., "Theories of revolution reconsidered: Contrasting models of collective violence," *Theory and Society*, vol. 8, no. 1, 1979, pp. 1–38.

Bacevich, A.J., "Hunkered down in Bosnia," *Weekly Standard*, 22 July 1996, pp. 12–14.

Baldwin, D., *Economic statecraft*, Princeton University Press, Princeton, 1985.

Baldwin, R, *Toward an integrated Europe*, Centre for Economic Policy Research, London, 1994.

Banac, I (ed.), *Eastern Europe in revolution*, Cornell University Press, Ithaca, 1992.

Banac, I., *The national question in Yugoslavia*, Cornell University Press, Ithaca, 1985.

Benedict, A., *Imagined communities: Reflections on the origins and spread of nationalism*, Verso, London, 1983.

Bercovitz, J.J., Anagnoson, T. & Wille, D.L., "Some conceptual issues and empirical trends in the study of successful mediation in relations," *Journal of Peace Research*, vol. 28, no. 1, 1991.

Berdal, M.R., "Fateful encounter: The United States and UN peacekeeping," *Survival*, vol. 36, no. 1, 1994, pp. 30–50.

Berdal, M.R., *Whither UN peacekeeping?* Adelphi Paper No. 281 IISS, London, 1993.

Betts, R.K., "The delusion of impartial intervention," *Foreign Affairs*, vol. 73, no. 6, 1994, pp. 20–33.
Betts, R.K., "Systems for peace or causes of war — Collective security, arms control, and the new Europe," *International Security*, vol. 17, no. 1, 1992, pp. 5–43.
Bildt, C., "Implementing the civilian tasks of the Bosnian Peace Accord," *NATO Review* 44/5, September 1996, pp. 3–6.
Bildt, C., "The prospects for Bosnia," *RUSI Journal* 141/1, December 1996, pp. 1–5.
Blackwill, R.D., "A taxonomy for defining US national security interests in the 1990s and beyond," in W. Weidenfeld and J. Janning (eds)., *Europe in global change: Strategies and options for Europe*, Bartelsmann Foundation, Gutersloh, 1993, pp. 100–19.
Borton, J., *NGOs and relief operations: Trends and policy implications*, Overseas Development Institute, London 1994.
Boutwell, J., Klare, M.T. & Reed, L.W. (eds)., *Lethal commerce: The global trade in small arms and light weapons* (Committee on International Security Studies, American Academy of Arts and Sciences, Cambridge, Mass., 1995.
Brown, M.E. (ed.), *The international dimensions of internal conflict*, MIT Press, Cambridge, Mass., 1996.
Brown, M.E. (ed.), *Ethnic conflict and international security*, Princeton University Press, Princeton, 1993.
Buchheit, L.C., *Secession: The legitimacy of self-determination*, Yale University Press, New Haven, 1978.
Bull, H., "Civil violence and international order," in *Civil violence and the international system*, Adelphi Paper No. 83 International Institute for Strategic Studies, London, 1971, pp. 27–36.
Čalić, M-J., "Bosnia and Herzegovina after Dayton: Chances and risks for peace", *Review of International Affairs*, no. 1046–47, July–August 1996, pp. 13–7.
Caryl, C., "Remember: No goose steps," *US News & World Report*, 21 October 1996, p. 56.
Chayes, A.H. & Chayes, A., "Regime architecture: Elements and principles," in Janne E. Nolan (ed.), *Global engagement: Cooperation and security in the 21st century*, Brookings Institution, Washington, 1994, pp. 65–130.
Chazan, N. (ed.), *Irredentism and international politics*, Lynne Rienner, Boulder, 1991.

Cohan, A.S., *Theories of revolution*, Wiley, New York, 1975.
Cohen, L., *Broken bonds: The disintegration of Yugoslavia*, Westview, Boulder, 1993.
Cot, J-P. & Pellet, A. (eds), *La Charte des Nations Unies, Commentaire article par article*, 2nd ed., Economica, Paris, 1991.
Cuthbertson, I., & Liebowitz, J., *Minorities: The new Europes's old issue*, Westview, Boulder, 1993.
Daalder, I., *The Clinton Administration and multilateral peace operations*, Draft Pew Case Study, August 1994.
Damrosch, L.F., "The civilian impact of economic sanctions," in L.F. Damrosch (ed.), *Enforcing restraint: Collective intervention in internal conflicts*, Council on Foreign Relations, New York, 1993, pp. 274–315.
Davis, M. (ed.), *Civil war and the politics of international relief*, Praeger, New York, 1975.
Day, E., *Economic sanctions imposed by the United States against specific countries: 1979 through 1992*, Congressional Research Service, Washington, 1992.
De Silva, K.M. & May, R.J. (eds), *Internationalization of ethnic conflict*, Pinter, London, 1991.
Diehl, P., *International peacekeeping*, Johns Hopkins University Press, Baltimore, 1993.
Dinstbier, J., *Sanjarenje o Evropi*, transl. from the Czech into Serbian by A. Ilić, Dečje novine, Gornji Milanovac, 1991.
Downs, G. (ed.), *Collective security beyond the Cold War*, University of Michigan Press, Ann Arbor, 1994.
Dupuy, R-J. (ed.), *Le developpement du role de Conseil du securite: The Development of the Role of the Security Council*, Hague Academy of International Law Workshop, The Hague, 21–23 July, 1992, Martinus Nijhoff, Dordrecht, 1993.
Durch, W.J. (ed.), *The evolution of UN peacekeeping: Case studies and comparative analysis*, St. Martin's, New York, 1993.
Eckstein, H. (ed.), *International war: Problems and approaches*, The Free Press, New York, 1964.
Edwards, M. & Hulme, D. (eds), *Making a difference: NGOs and development in a changing world*, Earthscan, London, 1992.
Eliot, K. & Hufbauer, G., "'New' Approaches to economic sanctions," in A. Kanter & L. Brooks (eds), *U. S. intervention policy for the post-Cold War world: New challenges and new responses*, American Assembly, New York, 1994, pp. 132–58.

Erlanger, S., "Bosnia uproar: Why U. S. pushes for early vote," *New York Times*, 12 June 1996, p. A3.
Esman, M.J. & Shibley, T. (eds), *International organizations and ethnic conflict*, Cornell University Press, Ithaca, 1995.
Esman, M.J., "Ethnic actors in international politics," *Nationalism and ethnic politics*, vol. 1, no. 1, Spring 1995, pp. 111–25.
Esman, M.J., *Ethnic politics*, Cornell University Press, Ithaca, 1994.
Esman, M.J. (ed.), *Ethnic conflict in the western world*, Cornell University Press, Ithaca, 1977.
Fatić, A., "Expansion in a ghastly light", *Peace and Security*, vol. XXX, March 1998, pp. 36–40.
Fatić, A., "Kosovo and eastern European democratization: Solving an indigestible problem", *Danubius*, no. 3/4, 1997, pp. 22–27.
Fatić, A., "Psychopathy: Cognitive aspects and criminal responsibility", *The Criminologist*, vol. 21, no. 2, 1997, pp. 64–75.
Fatić, A., *Crime and social control in central-eastern Europe: A guide to theory and practice*, Ashgate, Aldershot, 1997.
Fatić, A., "The need for a politically balanced work of The Hague International War Crimes Tribunal", *Review of International Affairs*, vol. XLVII, no. 1044, 1996, pp. 8–11.
Fein, H, "Explanations of genocide," *Current Sociology*, vol. 38, no. 1, 1990, pp. 32–50.
Freedman, L. (ed.), *Military intervention in European conflicts*, Blackwell, Oxford, 1994.
Freiherr von Richthofen, H., "Evolution of NATO from a German point of view," *RUSI Journal* 141/4, December 1996, pp. 39–44.
Gagnon, V.P., Jr., "Ethnic nationalism and international conflict: The case of Serbia," *International Security*, vol. 19, no. 3, 1994/95, pp. 130–66.
Glenny, M., *The fall of Yugoslavia: The Third Balkan War*, Penguin, London, 1992.
Goldstone, J.A., "Theories of revolution: The third generation," *World Politics*, vol. 32, no. 3, 1980, pp. 425–53.
Goodby, J., "Peacekeeping in the new Europe," *Washington Quarterly*, vol. 15, no. 2, 1992, pp. 153–71.
Goose, S.D. & Smyth, F., "Arming genocide in Rwanda," *Foreign Affairs*, vol. 73, no. 5, 1994, pp. 86–96.
Goulder, J., "NATO approaching two summits: The UK perspective," *RUSI Journal* 141/4, December 1996, pp. 29–32.

Graubard, S. (ed.), *Eastern Europe... Central Europe... Europe*, Oxford University Press, Oxford, 1993.
Gurr, T.R. & Harff, B., *Ethnic conflict and world politics*, Westview, Boulder, 1994.
Gurr, T.R., "Peoples against states: Ethnopolitical conflict and the changing world system," *International Studies Quarterly*, vol. 38, 1994, pp. 347–77.
Gurr, T.R., *Minorities at risk: A global view of ethnopolitical conflicts*, U.S. Institute of Peace Press, Washington, 1993.
Gurr, T.R., *Why men rebel*, Princeton University Press, Princeton, 1970.
Haas, E.B., "Regime decay: Conflict management and international organizations, 1945–1981," *International Organization*, vol. 37, no. 2, pp. 189–256.
Halperin, M., and Scheffer, D., *Self-determination in the new world order*, Carnegie Endowment for International Peace, Washington, 1992.
Hannum, H., *Autonomy, sovereignty, and self-determination: The accomodation of conflicting rights*, University of Pennsylvania Press, Philadelphia, 1990.
Hendrickson, D., "The democratic crusade: Intervention, economic sanctions and engagement," *World Policy Journal*, vol. 21, no. 4, 1994/95, pp. 18–30.
Heraclides, A., "Secessionist minorities and external involvement," *International Organization*, vol. 44, no. 3, 1990, pp. 341–78.
Hill, S. & Rothchild, D., "The contagion of political conflict in Africa and the world," *Journal of Conflict Resolution*, vol. 30, no. 4, 1986, pp. 716–35.
Horowitz, D.L., *Ethnic groups in conflict*, University of California Press, Berkeley, 1985.
Human Rights Watch, *Playing the "communal card": Communal violence and human rights*, Human Rights Watch, New York, 1995.
Huntington, S.P., "Civil violence and the process of development," in *Civil violence and the international system*, Adelphi Paper no. 83, IISS, London, 1971.
Huntington, S.P., *Political order in changing societies*, Yale University Press, New Haven, 1968.
Iveković, I., "Neopatrijarhat i političko nasilje: Prilog razumevanju etničkih sukoba na Balkanu i Kavkazu", *Republika*, no. 174, 1997, pp. I–XX.
James, A., *Peacekeeping in international politics*, St. Martin's, New York, 1990.

Johnsen, W.T., *U.S. participation in IFOR: A marathon, not a sprint*, Strategic Studies Institute, US Army War College, Carlisle Barracks, PA, 20 June 1996.

Kaempfer, W. & Lowenberg, A., *International economic sanctions: A public choice perspective*, Westview, Boulder, 1992.

Kampelman, M.M., "Secession and the right to self-determination: An urgent need to harmonize principle and practice," *Washington Quarterly*, vol. 16, no. 3, 1993, pp. 5–12.

Karp, A., "Arming ethnic conflict," *Arms Control Today*, vol. 23, no. 7, 1993, pp. 8–13.

Karp, R.C. (ed), *Central and eastern Europe: The challenge of transition*, Oxford University Press, Oxford, 1993.

Kent, R., *Anatomy of disaster relief: The international network in action*, Puster, London, 1987.

Klare, M.T., "Awash in armaments: Implications of the trade in light weapons," *Harvard International Review*, vol. 17, no. 1, 1994/95, pp. 24–26, 75–76.

Korten, D., *Getting to the 21st century: Voluntary action and the global agenda*, Kumarian, Hartford, 1990.

Kuper, L., *Genocide: Its political use in the twentieth century*, Yale University Press, New Haven, 1981.

Lake, A., "Bosnia after Dayton," *U.S. Department of State Dispatch*, 24 June 1996, pp. 330–2.

Leyton-Brown, D. (ed.), *The utility of international economic sanctions*, St. Martin's, New York, 1987.

Licklider, R. (ed.), *Stopping the killing: How civil wars end*, New York University Press, New York, 1993.

Little, R., *Intervention: External involvement in civil wars*, Rowman and Littlefield, Totowa, 1975.

Lowe, V. & Warbrick, C. (eds), *The United Nations and the principles of international law*, Routledge, London, 1994.

Luard, E. (ed.), *The international regulation of civil wars*, Thames and Hudson, London, 1972.

Martin, L., *Coercive cooperation*, Princeton University Press, Princeton, 1992.

McCarthy, K.D., Hodgkinson, V., Samariwalla, R. et al., *The nonprofit sector in the global community*, Jossey Bass, San Francisco, 1992.

Miall, H. (ed.), *Minority rights in Europe: Prospects for a transnational regime*, Royal Institute of International Affairs, London, 1994.

Midlarsky, M.I. (ed.), *The internationalization of communal strife*, Routledge, London, 1992.
Minear, L. et al., *Humanitarian action in the Former Yugoslavia: The UN's role 1991-1993*, Occasional Paper No. 18, Watson Institute for International Studies, Providence, 1994.
Minear, L., and Weiss, T.G., *Mercy under fire: War and the global humanitarian community*, Westview, Boulder, 1995.
Miyagwa, M., *Do economic sanctions work?*, St. Martin's, New York, 1992.
Modelski, G., "International settlement of internal war," in J.N. Rosenau (ed.), *International aspects of civil strife*, Princeton University Press, Princeton, 1964, pp. 122–53.
Montville, J.V. (ed.), *Conflict and peacekeeping in multiethnic societies*, Lexington Books, Lexington, 1990.
Myers, S.L., "U. S. and NATO plan new Bosnia force," *New York Times*, 26 October 1996, p. 1.
Neville-Jones, P., "Dayton, IFOR and alliance relations in Bosnia," *Survival* 38/4, 1996/7, pp. 44–65.
Newhouse, J., "No exit, no entrance," *New Yorker*, 28 June 1993, pp. 44–51.
Newhouse, J., "Dodging the problem," *New Yorker*, 24 August 1992, pp. 60–71.
Newman, S., "Does modernization breed ethnic political conflict?" *World Politics*, vol. 43, no. 3, 1991, pp. 451–78.
Nordlinger, E.A., *Conflict regulation in divided societies*, Harvard University, Center for International Affairs, Cambridge, Mass., 1972.
O'Connor, M., "Target for hostage-takers: U. N. unit," *New York Times*, 17 July 1996, p. A8.
Perlez, J., "Officer says NATO can seize Serbs if ordered to," *New York Times*, 22 June 1996, p. A5.
Pomfret, J., "Perry sees longer U. S. role in Bosnia," *Washington Post*, 13 June 1996, p. A24.
Popović, M., *Politički aparthejd: Balkanska postmoderna 3*, Monitor, Podgorica, 1997.
Posen, B.R., "The security dilemma and ethnic conflict," in M.E. Brown (ed.), *Ethnic conflict and international security*, Princeton University Press, Princeton, 1993, pp. 103–24.
Randell, J. & German, T. (eds), *The reality of aid 94*, Actionaid, London, 1994.

Reed, L.W. & Kaysen, C., *Emerging norms of justified intervention*, American Academy of Arts and Sciences, Cambridge, Mass., 1993.
Reisman, W.M., "Peacemaking," *Yale Journal of International Law*, vol. 18, no. 1, 1993, pp. 415–22.
Renwick, R., *Economic sanctions*, Harvard University, Center for International Affairs, Cambridge, Mass., 1981.
Rieff, D., "In Bosnia, a prelude to partition," *New York Times*, 14 August 1996, p. A21.
Rikhye, I.J., *The theory and practice of peacekeeping*, C. Hurst and Company for the International Peace Academy, London, 1984.
Roberts, A. & Kingsbury, B. (eds), *United Nations, divided world: The UN's role in international relations*, 2nd ed., Clarendon Press, Oxford, 1993.
Rodman, K.A., "Sanctions at bay? Hegemonic decline, multinational corporations, and U. S. economic sanctions since the pipeline case," *International Organization*, vol. 49, no. 1, 1995, p. 105–37.
Rollo, J, & Smith, A., "EC trade with eastern Europe," *Economic Policy*, no. 16, 1993, pp. 140–81.
Ronzitti, N., *Rescuing nationals abroad and intervention on the grounds of humanity*, Martinus Nijhoff, Dordrecht, 1985.
Rosenau, J.N. (ed.), *International aspects of civil strife*, Princeton University Press, Princeton, 1964.
Rothchild, D. & Groth, A.J., "Pathological dimensions of domestic and international ethnicity," *Political Science Quarterly*, vol. 110, no. 1, 1995, pp. 69–82.
Rothchild, J., *Ethnopolitics: A conceptual framework*, Columbia University Press, New York, 1981.
Rule, J.B., *Theories of civil violence*, University of California Press, Berkeley, 1988.
Samarasinghe, S.W.R. de A. & Coughlin, R. (eds), *Economic dimensions of ethnic conflict*, Pinter, London, 1991.
Schneider, B., *Barefoot revolution: A report to the club of Rome*, IT Publications, Rome, 1988.
Schopflin, G., *Hungary and its neighbors*, Chaillot Paper No. 7, Western European Union, Institute for Security Studies, Paris, May 1993.
Sharp, J.M.O., "Doing better on Bosnia: Enforce the law, protect rights," *The World Today* 53/2, 1997 pp. 37–9.
Shehadi, K.S., *Ethnic self-determination and the break-up of states*, Adelphi Paper No. 283, IISS, London, 1993.

Smith, A. & Wallace, H., "The new European Union: Towards a policy for Europe," *International Affairs*, vol. 70, no. 3, 1994, pp. 429–44.
Smith, A.D., *National identity*, Penguin, London, 1991.
Smith, A.D., *The ethnic origins of nations*, Basil Blackwell, New York, 1986.
Smith, A.D., *The ethnic revival in the modern world*, Cambridge University Press, New York, 1981.
Smith, B.H., *More than altruism: The politics of private foreign aid*, Princeton University Press, Princeton, 1990.
Smith, L.W., Jr., "The pillars of peace in Bosnia," *NATO Review* 44/4, 1996, pp. 11–6.
Spiro, P.J., "New global communities: Nongovernmental organizations in international decision-making institutions," *Washington Quarterly*, vol. 18, no. 1, 1995, pp. 45–56.
"Statute of the International Tribunal for the Prosecution of Persons Responsible for Serious Violations of International Humanitarian Law Committed in the Territory of the Former Yugoslavia since 1991", in *Basic Documents*, The United Nations — International Criminal Tribunal for the Former Yugoslavia, The Hague, 1995. pp. 489–535.
Stedman, S.J., "UN intervention in civil wars: Imperatives of choice and stragety," in D.C.F. Daniel & B.C. Hayes (eds), *Beyond traditional peacekeeping*, St. Martin's, New York, 1995, pp. 40–63.
Stedman, S.J., *Peacemaking in civil war: International mediation in Zimbabwe, 1974–1980*, Lynne Rienner, Boulder, 1991.
Steinberg, J., "Yugoslavia," in L.F. Damrosch (ed.), *Enforcing restraint: Collective intervention in internal conflicts*, Council on Foreign Relations, New York, 1993, pp. 27–76.
Thakur, R.,"Human rights: Amnesty International and the United Nations," *Journal of Peace Research*, vol. 31, no. 2, 1994, pp. 143–60.
The Clinton Administration's policy on reforming multilateral peace operations, PDD–25, The White House Press Office, May 1994.
The Dayton Peace Accords, as released by the US Department of State Foreign Affairs Network, Internet edition, http://dosfan.lib.uic.edu, Office of Public Communications, Bureau of Public Affairs, US Department of State, 1995.
"The path to The Hague: Selected documents on the origins of the International Criminal Tribunal for the Former Yugoslavia, internet edition, www.un.org/icty.

Tilly, C., "Does modernization breed revolution?" *Comparative Politics*, vol. 5, no. 3, 1973, pp. 425–47.
Touval, S., "Why the UN fails," *Foreign Affairs*, vol. 73, no. 5, 1994, pp. 44–57.
United Nations Institute for Disarmament Research (UNIDIR), "Peace-keeping, peace-making, Peace enforcement," *UNIDIR Newsletter*, no. 24, December 1993.
United Nations, *The blue helmets: A review of United Nations peace-keeping*, United Nations, New York, 1990.
Van Evera, S., "Hyphothesis on nationalism and war," *International Security*, vol. 18, no. 4, 1994, pp. 5–39.
Van Evera, S., "Primed for peace: Europe after the Cold War," *International Security*, vol. 15, no. 3, 1990/91, pp. 7–57.
Von Hippel, K., "The resurgence of nationalism and its international implications," *Washington Quarterly*, vol. 14, no. 4, 1994, pp. 185–200.
Vukadinović, R., "The enlargement of NATO and the countries of former Yugoslavia", *Peace and Security*, vol. XXIX, September 1997, pp. 13–23.
Wainhouse, D.W., *International peace observation: A history and forecast*, Johns Hopkins University Press, Baltimore, 1966.
Walt, S.M., "Revolution and war," *World Politics*, vol. 44, no. 3, 1992, pp. 321–68.
Walter, B.F., "The resolution of civil wars: Why negotiations fail," Ph.D. dissertation, University of Chicago, 1994.
Walters, F.P., *A history of the League of Nations*, Oxford University Press, London, 1952.
Waltz, K.N., *Man, the state and war: A theoretical analysis*, Columbia University Press, New York, 1959.
Watson, M., *Contemporary minority nationalism*, Routledge, London, 1990.
Weiner, M., "Peoples and states in a new ethnic order?" *Third World Quarterly*, vol. 13, no. 2, 1992, pp. 317–33.
Weiss, T.G., Forsythe, D.P. & Coate, R.A., *The United Nations and changing world politics*, Westview, Boulder, 1994.
Weiss, T.G. (ed.), *NGOs, the UN, and global governance*, Lynne Rienner, Boulder, 1996.
Weiss, T.G. (ed.), *The United Nations and civil wars*, Lynne Rienner, Boulder, 1995.

Weller, M., "The international response to the dissolution of the Socialist Federal Republic of Yugoslavia," *American Journal of International Law*, vol. 86, no. 3, 1992, pp. 569–607.

White, N.D., *Keeping the peace: The United Nations and the maintenance of international peace and security*, Manchester University Press, Manchester, 1993.

Whitefield, S. (ed.), *The new institutional architecture of eastern Europe*, Macmillan, London, 1993.

Wilkinson, T., "'Factions' resistance may doom Bosnia pact, top officer says," *Los Angeles Times*, 8 June 1996, p. A3

Williams, C.H., *National separatism*, University of Wales Press, Cardiff, 1982.

Wurst, J., "Mozambique disarms," *Bulletin of the Atomic Scientists*, vol. 50, no. 5, 199), pp. 36–9.

Zametica, J., *The Yugoslav conflict*, Adelphi Paper No. 270, IISS, London, 1992.

Zartman, I.W. (ed.), *Collapsed states: The disintegration and restoration of legitimate authority*, Lynne Rienner, Boulder, 1995.

Zartman, I.W., *Ripe for resolution: Conflict and intervention in Africa*, 2nd ed., Oxford University Press, New York, 1989.

Zimmerman, W., "The last Ambassador," *Foreign Affairs*, vol. 74, no. 2, 1995, pp. 2–20.